BEHI
STEELE DOSSIER

In Simpson's Own Words...

Full U.S. Senate Judiciary Committee Examination
*and other under oath answers from FBI * CIA * DOJ*

Written by: **Daniel David Elles**
A Forgotten American from Macomb County, MI

With thanks: **To all attorneys in the Exam:**
They all truly did non-partisan work for our United States to provide much needed answers. Especially:
Heather Sawyer, Chief Oversight Counsel, Senator Feinstein – Ranking Member
Patrick Davis, Deputy Chief Investigative Counsel, Chairman Grassley

---

Walt Whitman wrote in "Democratic Vistas" (1871):

Never was there, perhaps, more hollowness at heart
than at present,
and here in the United States....
Genuine belief seems to have left us.
The underlying principles of the States are not honestly believ'd in,..
nor is humanity itself believ'd in.
What penetrating eye does not everywhere see through the mask?
The spectacle is appalling.

VOLUME I.

Copyright © 2018 Daniel David Elles.

Publication Date:	28 February 2018	Updated: 16 Aug 2018
ISBN-10:	0-9968863-7-0	
ISBN-13:	978-0-9968863-7-6	
Library of Congress:	2018909559	U.S. Copyright Office

Published by: Tiber Publishing

400 Renaissance Center, Suite 2600
Detroit, Michigan 48243

www.TiberPublishing.com
www.DanielDavidElles.com

Daniel@TiberPublishing.com
Daniel.david.elles@GMAIL.COM

The author and/or contributors are not responsible for, and should not be deemed to endorse or recommend, any product or website other than his own. The author and contributors, similarly, cannot be responsible for third party material and articles from other publications. The author has made every attempt to accurately describe the publicly posted and/or broadcasted quotes from public figures, the press, government officials, congressional testimony, court filings, and other noteworthy sources. He takes no credit for their words, quotes, articles and/or opinions. He is not responsible for their accuracy.

In 2010, the author qualified to be on the Michigan House of Representatives as an "Independent" in MACOMB COUNTY.

PAGES 90 – 202 IS THE
FULL SIMPSON SENATE EXAM

CERTIFICATE OF SHORTHAND REPORTER - NOTARY PUBLIC

I, TINA M. ALFARO, Certified Shorthand Reporter No. 084-004220, Certified Real-time Reporter, and Notary Public in and for the State of Illinois, do hereby certify:

That **GLENN SIMPSON,** whose interview is hereinbefore set forth, was duly sworn by me and that said deposition is a true record of the testimony given by such witness.

I further certify that I am not counsel for nor in any way related to any of the parties to this suit, nor am I in any way interested in the outcome thereof.

**"I don't know whether or not such collusion -- and that's your term, such collusion existed.
I don't know.**

Former CIA Director Brennan –
HPSCI Hearing – 14 NOV 2017
Answer to Rep. Gowdy (R-SC)

**"He (Steele) was
'horrified and remains horrified that the US Defendants (Buzzfeed) published the dossier at all...
such publication of such raw intelligence reports in this way is unthinkable.'"**

Senior Master Fontaine –
QUEEN'S BENCH DIVISION
Case No: CR 2017 - 664

CONTENTS

"Did you do any independent verification of these (dossier) facts?"

Heather Sawyer – Chief Oversight Counsel,
Sen. Feinstein (D-CA)

"I can't talk about this as a verification, but...I analyzed this information in the same manner I analyzed the other stuff."

Glenn R. Simpson –
Founder & CEO, Fusion GPS

"I think it's safe to say that, you know, at some point probably early in 2016,

I had reached a conclusion about Donald Trump as a businessman and his character and
I was opposed to Donald Trump."

Glenn R. Simpson – Founder & CEO Fusion GPS

TRUMP COLLUSION?

On 22 AUGUST 2017, Fusion GPS Founder and CEO, Glenn Simpson, appeared for an under oath Senate Examination. Below is a summary (see last chapter) where Simpson makes some interesting conclusions regarding his research on then Candidate Trump. And, after Mueller's Special Counsel has yet to find any collusion that we know of, I thought it would be best to summarize what Glenn Simpson and Christopher Steele concluded in their comprehensive quest for "conspiracy."

This exchange is between Heather Sawyer – Chief Oversight Counsel for Diane Feinstein (D-CA) – and Simpson:

Q: So in May or June 2016 you hired Christopher Steele to, as you've just indicated, find out what he could about Donald Trump's business activities in Russia. Did something trigger that assignment?

A: No, I don't think I could point to something in particular as a trigger. I mean, the basis for the request (to hire Steele) was he (Trump) had made a number of trips to Russia and talked about doing a number of business deals but never did one, and that struck me as a little bit odd and calling for an explanation.

Q: I think what I'm trying to get some sense of comfort around is to the extent there might be concerns that the work being done was driven in a direction designed to reach a particular conclusion for a client or because of the client's identity was that the case?

A: I think it's safe to say that, you know, at some point probably early in 2016 I had reached a conclusion about Donald Trump as a businessman and his character and I was opposed to Donald Trump.
So most of what I do as a research person is we try to avoid getting into situations where one's etiology or political views would cloud your work because it's a known hazard, but, you know, I reached an opinion about Donald Trump and his suitability **to be president of**

the United States and I was concerned about whether he was the best person for the job.

Q: And given that you had been trained not to allow etiology to cloud your work, it sounds like you reached a conclusion and had concerns about Candidate Trump. What steps did you take to then ensure that your conclusion didn't cloud the work that was being done?

A: Well, to be clear, my concerns were in the category of character and competence rather than -- I didn't have any specific concerns for much of the time about his views, which I don't share, but that wasn't really the issue. Most of what we do has to do with do people have integrity and whether they've been involved in **illicit activity**. So those were the things I focused on.

Q: You mentioned that earlier and I think you made clear a number of times in the course of the day that the specific work **on Russian interference and possible ties to the campaign** that Mr. Steele was doing was one part of that bigger picture...In particular one of the things you had mentioned -- well, you just mentioned right now as we were speaking the term "illicit activity."

What, if any, research did you conduct that gave you any concerns about then Candidate Trump and potential illicit activity?

A: I think the thing I cited to you was his relationship with organized crime figures, and that was a concern.

Q: And what can you share with us about the findings, your findings?

A: --As I say, there were **various allegations** of fraudulent business practices or dishonest business practices or connections with organized crime figures...

Q: Did you feel in the course of that that you had uncovered evidence of any criminal activity by Donald Trump?

A: In the course of that I don't think so. I think my concern was the associations with known organized crime figures.

For the Forgotten Americans

"Did any of that indicate anything that showed a connection to Russia or the Russian government or Russian officials or Russian oligarchs?"

Heather Sawyer–
Chief Oversight Counsel, Sen. Feinstein (D-CA)

"Not that I can recall."

Glenn R. Simpson
Founder & CEO, Fusion GPS

Q: You mentioned as well that you had reviewed tax bills. Were these specifically Donald Trump's tax bills?

A: They were Trump properties and I believe we may have reviewed some public information about estate taxes and things like that. We didn't have access to his tax returns.

Q: Did you reach any conclusions based on your review of his tax bills? I think you mentioned that in connection with trying to assess either financial connections or his financial standing. Did you reach any conclusions with regard to either of those?

A: Yes. I concluded -- we concluded that his statements about what individual properties were worth were greatly exaggerated and at odds with the information that he'd supplied, you know, in legal filings with tax authorities and other records, corporate records.

Q: <u>Did any of that indicate anything that showed a connection to Russia or the Russian government or Russian officials or Russian oligarchs?</u>

A: **Not that I can recall.**

Q: You brought up Trump golf courses. What in particular were you looking into with regard to Donald Trump's golf courses?

A: The original inquiry was into the value of the courses, whether he had to borrow money to buy them, whether they were encumbered with debt, how much money they brought in, what valuations...

Q: Can you share what findings and conclusions you reached?

A: A number of them don't make any money. His valuations of the properties are questionable. I guess those would be the main findings.

Q: You just mentioned broadly but didn't describe it, you mentioned research on Scotland... Can you just describe what that research was.

A: Sure. He has golf courses in Scotland and Ireland and one of the facets of UK or Anglo company law is that private companies have to file financial statements, public financial statements.

"Did you feel in the course of that that you had uncovered evidence of any <u>criminal activity</u> by Donald Trump?"

Sawyer

"In the course of that I don't think so."

Simpson

So when you're looking at a guy like Donald Trump who doesn't like to share information about his company, it's useful to find a jurisdiction where he's required to share that information with the local government.

So we went and ordered the records – the financial statements of the golf courses. There's also a long-running land use controversy -- I think there's multiple long-running land use controversies over those properties...

Q: With regard to the public financial statements, did you reach any conclusions based on that?

A: That they were not profitable entities.

I don't specifically recall. I just remember that these were not doing very well and that he'd sunk a lot of money into them and he hadn't gotten a lot of money back yet.

Q: And with regard to that work, did you share any of that information with law enforcement agencies?

A: No. I mean, just to reiterate, the only contact that, you know, occurred during this engagement was -- at least to my knowledge, was Chris's dealing with the FBI. Other than that, I don't remember having any dealings with the FBI.

THE DOSSIER & MUELLER

Law enforcement will make deals with a killer when there is someone behind it (i.e. the person who paid for the hit).

Why? Because, therein, lies the details behind the homicide and the motives are revealed. IF not but for, the person behind the murder, the killing would have never occurred. The person who pulled the trigger was just a means to the end.

The same holds true with The Steele Dossier.

Its author, Christopher Steele, is simply the person who wrote the document ("pulled the trigger"). To understand The Steele Dossier it is essential, no it's imperative, to know the reasons it was written and the rationale behind it. Much has been said about the document, but nobody has accumulated 1,500 pages of under oath testimony about The Steele Dossier...**until now**!

This book was first published 27 February 2018 on Amazon. And, the May 2018 media hoopla about the FBI having an "INSIDER" on the Trump Campaign was fully covered back then!

How did I know? Because I read over 600 pages of Congressional testimony from the person responsible for hiring Steele – Glenn R. Simpson, Founder and CEO of Fusion GPS. In fact, his 8 hour Senate Exam is included in this book (*pg 90-202*).

Moreover, I had also stated that the *HPSCI Minority Memo* (*Correcting the Record – The Russia Investigation*) "may be wrong". Six months later, that Memo has, in fact, been proven to be rather misleading. For example, it's hard to believe that:

*Christopher Steele's raw intelligence reporting did <u>not</u> inform the FBI's decision to initiate its counterintelligence investigation in late July 2016...In fact, the FBI's closely-held investigative team only received Steele's reporting in mid-September – **more than seven weeks later***

<u>INDICTMENTS FROM THE DOSSIER</u>

Today, August 16, 2018, many of the indictments by Special Counsel Mueller's team and/or the DOJ are persons named in Simpson's Congressional testimonies (22 AUG 2017 at the Senate and 14 NOV 2017 at the House). Simpson says:

- **<u>Maria Butina</u>** – (waiting for trial)

  Maria Butina, also was a big Trump fan in Russia, and then suddenly showed up here and started hanging around the Trump transition after the election and rented an apartment and enrolled herself at AU (American University), which I assume gets you a visa...I think she is suspicious.

- **<u>Paul Manafort</u>** – (in court)

  I knew a lot about Paul Manafort from my career at The Wall Street Journal...I had written a number of stories about his involvement with Oleg Deripaska and the pro-Russia party in Ukraine and another oligarch named Firtash.

  And some Paul Manafort shell company accounts wound up I think at the Bank of Cyprus.

  We learned of his relationship with Ukrainian and Russian oligarchs....He was subject of some litigation over his business dealings in New York.

- **<u>Michael Cohen</u>** – (raided and investigated)

  We gradually began to understand more about Michael Cohen, the President's lawyer, and his background, and that he had a lot of connections to the former Soviet Union, and that he seemed to have associations with organized crime figures in New York and Florida, Russian organized crime...There was Simon Garber, the taxi king.

  ...people told us he (COHEN) spoke Russian. And his father-in-law is from Ukraine. He seems to have a lot of business dealings over there.

- **Carter Page** – (The FBI remains silent)

Oops! He hasn't been indicted. But there are "allegations".

Nevertheless, as the suspected Russian spy, Carter Page, continues to roam free and conducts various interviews, he remains a central figure in this whole Russian Collusion Conspiracy with the Trump Campaign.

Below are brief excerpts from the US Senate, along with The Steele Dossier memos and what Simpson said in his testimony:

✓ **U.S. Senate Judiciary Committee – Grassley-Graham Memo.**

The documents we have reviewed show that the FBI took important investigative steps largely based on Mr. Steele's information-and relying heavily on his credibility. Specifically, on October 21, 2016, the FBI filed its first warrant application under FISA for Carter Page.

The bulk of the application consists of allegations against Page that were disclosed to the FBI by Mr. Steele and are also outlined in the Steele dossier. The application appears to contain no additional information corroborating the dossier allegations against Mr. Page, although it does cite to a news article that appears to be sourced to Mr. Steele's dossier as well

✓ **STEELE DOSSIER:**

- TRUMP advisor Carter PAGE holds secret meetings in Moscow with SECHIN and senior Kremlin Internal Affairs official, DIVYEKIN.
- SECHIN raises issues of future bilateral US-Russia energy co-operation ...PAGE non-committal in response.
- Substance included offer of large stake in Rosneft in return for lifting on Russia PAGE confirms this is TRUMP"s intention
- Paul MANAFORT, who was using foreign policy advisor, Carter PAGE, and others as (Kremlin) intermediaries.
- Kremlin engaging with several high profile players, STEIN, PAGE

✓ SIMPSON SAYS:

"**Chris (Steele) identified Carter Page as someone who had -- <u>seemed</u> to be in the middle of the campaign, between the Trump campaign and the Kremlin**, and he later turned out to be an espionage suspect who was, in fact, someone that the FBI had been investigating for years. … we got the Carter Page information, which was, you know, gee, we will never- **I will never find a way to confirm whether he talked to Igor Sechin,** but what was he doing in Moscow at this school…"

"And I can remember specifically there being stories about Carter Page and his trip to Moscow and the fact that that was something that was of FBI interest, and **that Carter Page stuff is something that we covered with the media.**"

"So anyway, in the course of reading up on my espionage cases, I found a case involving a guy named Buryakov…And then in the prosecution, they identified people that he was trying to recruit. And one of the guys fit the description of Carter Page. And so eventually, you know, a reporter asked Carter Page, Hey, is this you, and he said yes. And so, you know, I mean in terms of like things that have turned to be accurate about the dossier, I mean like, okay, so this guy seems like a zero, but, in fact, you know, in espionage tradecraft, you know, you are not going to target, you know, someone with a good job and a stable family and a long work history, because they are going to tell you to get lost. But you are going to target someone who is greedy, lonely, ambitious."

The point of this piece on Carter Page is that The Steele Dossier asserts, and Simpson claims, that Page was "in the middle the campaign, between the Trump campaign and the Kremiln". Yet, the HPSCI Minority Memo states that it (The Steele Dossier) had no bearing on the FISA Warrants.

Nothing was verified. There were **allegations – not facts!**

"But there is substantial evidence suggesting that Mr. Steele materially misled the FBI about a key aspect of his dossier efforts, one which bears on his credibility."

Chairman Grassley – Senate Judiciary Committee

CREDIBLE & RELIABLE

"We're going to present to you things that we think come from credible sources, but we're not going to warrant to you that what we - that this is -- that this is all true."

That was a Simpson quote to Democrat Congressman Quigley on how Steele discusses his research with clients. Below are few excerpts from his HPSCI – House Permanent Select Committee on Intelligence – Hearing with Congressmen Quigley (D-IL), Thomas Rooney (R-PA), and Trey Gowdy (R-SC):

MR. QUIGLEY: Did you have to do any other due diligence or what did you know about him (Steele) and his reputation before?

MR. SIMPSON: Chris (Steele) was a reliable provider of information that turned out to be reliable.

QUIGLEY: He said it was <u>raw data</u>. Is that correct?

SIMPSON: Yeah.

MR. QUIGLEY: In some respect?

SIMPSON: It's HUMINT, right? It's human source information...And humans sometimes lie, and more frequently they just get it wrong.

QUIGLEY: Did he ever, in talking to you subsequent to the release of the document, say that he thought he would alter any of it after the fact or information he had gathered later?

SIMPSON: I have - I have talked to him about that. And he remains -- he continues to believe that it is <u>largely</u> not disinformation.

ROONEY: So you just trusted Mr. Steele's vouch?

SIMPSON: I have great trust in Mr. Steele's professional ability to find sources with credible information.

ROONEY: Did you know how he paid these sources?

SIMPSON: To my knowledge, Chris does not pay sources for information.

ROONEY: So they give it up for free?

SIMPSON: When you're running a source network, essentially what you are doing is paying subcontractors to –

ROONEY: Right.

SIMPSON: -- circulate and gather information in conversations...So what I think the misconception is, is that, you know, Chris calls people up and says, "I'll give you $5,000 if you tell me what's going on with the Trump operation." And that didn't happen.

ROONEY: Are you sure?

SIMPSON: I've asked Chris about it, he said it doesn't--didn't happen.

GOWDY: Can you give me an example of something that he produced to you that you found to be not credible?

SIMPSON: No, I don't think anything comes to mind.

GOWDY: Is there anything that Steele, his sources or subsources told you that you didn't include because you immediately found it to be incredible? And I think your answer was no.

SIMPSON: That is correct. My answer to that is no.

GOWDY: How were you able to assess the accuracy of the information, the underlying information he provided you?

SIMPSON: I'm sorry; I thought you asked me whether there was anything in there that I found to be wrong.

GOWDY: I did.

SIMPSON: I haven't found anything to be wrong. If you'd like me to get into more of the corroboration, I can do that.

"In British intelligence, the methodology's a little different from American intelligence. There's a practice of being faithful to what people say. "

"So the more exotic the topic, the harder it is to find someone who doesn't sell you BS...
if they can't find anything out, they'll just make it up."

Glenn R. Simpson – Founder & CEO Fusion GPS

CORROBORATION

In answering Congressman Quigley, Simpson says:

SIMPSON: Sure. So basically the way the information biz works is, you know, it's a tricky business. A lot of it is about talent spotting, finding people that are reliable, produce reliable information. There's a lot of, I don't know if I'd call it fraud, but there's a lot of BS where people tell you stuff that doesn't turn out to be right. And so, you know, it's sort of like, again, being a journalist, where you're trying to figure out who your reliable sources are.

So the more exotic the topic, the harder it is to find someone who doesn't sell you BS. And, you know, one of the problems with the business is that basically if you contract with a guy to go find something out or go look into a subject, he doesn't – he rarely comes back and says: I got nothing for you, I wasn't able to find anything out. They'll just-- if they can't find anything out, they'll just make it up. So sorry for the long answer.

GOWDY: Were you able to vet or corroborate or contradict any of the sources or subsources?

SIMPSON: We did get into assessing the credibility of the sources and whether they were in a position to know the things that they were saying. I didn't ask for the specific identities of specific people...So the people, I think I know who they are for other reasons.

When the first reports came in, we did a lot of discussing of whether this was credible information.

And obviously, evaluating human Intelligence is not the same thing as looking at documents. And so it's a much trickier process and the thresholds are different. What you're really trying to do, which is kind of like interviewing in journalism, is figure out whether there's reason to think that what's being said is credible. And so we did a lot of that.

ROONEY: Do you - did you find anything to -- that you verified as false in the dossier, since or during?

SIMPSON: I have not seen anything –

ROONEY: So everything in that dossier, as far as you're concerned, is true or could be true?

SIMPSON: I didn't say that. What I said was it was credible at the time it came in. We were able to corroborate various things that supported its credibility.

ROONEY: Well, do you know now if anything's false?

SIMPSON: I did answer that. No, I don't know if anything is false.

ROONEY: Okay. Did you or anyone else independently verify or corroborate any information in the dossier? This is sort of a repeat of a question I just asked, but we're talking about verification here.

SIMPSON: Yes. Well, numerous things in the dossier have been verified. You know, I don't have access to the intelligence or law enforcement information that I see made reference to, but, you know, things like, you know, the Russian Government has been investigating Hillary Clinton and has a lot of information about her and is -- and the Trump people are interested in getting that information.

I mean, that turned out to be true. It was also true, you know -- I mean, if you just think back to the chronology of this, when the original memos came in saying that the Kremlin was mounting a specific operation to get Donald Trump elected President, that was not what the Intelligence Community was saying. The Intelligence Community was saying they are just seeking to disrupt our election and our political process, and that this is sort of kind of just a generally nihilistic, you know, trouble-making operation. And, you know, Chris turned out to be right, it was specifically designed to elect Donald Trump President.

For the Forgotten Americans

"We were encouraging the media to ask questions about whether the FBI was, in fact, investigating these matters...

so that they could go to the FBI and ask them if both candidates were under investigation.

Glenn R. Simpson – Founder & CEO Fusion GPS

THE MEDIA

Christopher Steele expresses his outrage in London cases: QUEEN'S HIGH BENCH Claim: HQ 17D00413 & CR2017-664.

According to Steele's sworn statements, the Dossier was <u>never</u> meant for publication. Senior Master Fontaine IN THE HIGH COURT OF JUSTICE wrote:

"The dossier consists of a number of memoranda produced by Mr. Steel and/or his company, Orbis Business Intelligence. Mr. Steele's evidence is that he was <u>"horrified and remains horrified that the US Defendants ("Buzzfeed") published the dossier at all</u>, let alone without substantial redactions...He says that...**such publication of such raw intelligence reports in this way is unthinkable.**"

Moreover, not only did the HPSCI Minority Memo state that the Steele Dossier was "raw intelligence", but FBI Director Comey's under oath testimony stated that The Steele Dossier was "salacious and unverified". And, that was not some "off-the-cuff" remark. Comey wrote those words in his prepared "Statement for the Record" at his 08 June 2017 Senate hearing.

Nevertheless, both Simpson and Steele briefed the media as to the memoranda's contents. And, the media ate it up faster than a third-grader devouring an ice cream cone.

In the London court, Senior Master Fontaine states: "Mr. Steele has been content to talk to journalists about the dossier".

And, Steele also signed a sworn statement: "Second Defendant (Steele) gave off the record briefings to a small number of journalists about the pre-election memoranda in late summer/autumn 2016".

For me, and most Americans, "late summer/autumn 2016" means between August and November. However, regarding the press briefings, Simpson states under oath:

> ...it (press briefings) was sometime in September or October.
>
> ...there were two instances of this or rounds of it...the first round was, I assume was sometime in mid-September or early October.
>
> ...we were encouraging the media to ask questions about whether the FBI was, in fact, investigating these matters.
>
> ... to give the press enough info so that they could go to the FBI and ask them if both candidates were under investigation....

There are two main points to this:

1. That they were briefing the press on "raw intelligence that was considered "salacious and unverified".
2. That, if the media briefings were held in the late summer, then this puts a huge dent into the beginning of the FBI investigation that began 31 JUL 2016 and the entire timeline.

- **CIA DIRECTOR BRENNAN:** "Sometime this summer (2016), there was (counterintelligence) information that CIA had that was shared with the Bureau".

- **Russian-American Akhmetshin** testified that "he began hearing from journalists about the dossier before it was published, and thought it was the summer of 2016".

Whether Simpson and Steele briefed the press in July or not, the fact is that the media and the FBI had the information. In the QUEEN'S BENCH DIVISION case, Senior Master Fontaine writes:

> Mr. Steele has been content to talk to journalists about the dossier; by way of example: Articles in Mother Jones dated 31st October 2016, and 13th January 2017; from those articles it is apparent that pre-election memos have been provided to a journalist at Mother Jones, David Corn.

At the Senate Exam, Glenn Simpson was questioned by Chairman Grassley's Chief Investigative Counsel, Jason Foster, and his Deputy Chief Investigative Counsel, Patrick Davis.

BY MR. DAVIS:

Q: I'm going to have you take a look at one of the filings by Mr. Steele's attorneys in the lawsuit against him and Orbis in the United Kingdom. This will be Exhibit 4. (Exhibit 4 was marked for identification.)

If you could please turn to page 2 and read paragraph No. 8. That paragraph states

> *At all material times Fusion was subject to an obligation not to disclose to third parties confidential intelligence material provided to it by the Defendants in the course of that working relationship without the agreement of the Defendants."*

Is that a correct description of your understanding of how the material was to be treated?

A: I'm not sure I can answer this--I'm not sure I know the answer to this.

IN THE HIGH COURT OF JUSTICE
QUEEN'S BENCH DIVISION

Claim No. HQ17D00413

-4 APR 2017

BETWEEN:-

(1) ALEKSEJ GUBAREV
(2) WEBZILLA B.V.
(3) WEBZILLA LIMITED
(4) XBT HOLDINGS S.A.

Claimants

-and-

(1) ORBIS BUSINESS INTELLIGENCE LIMITED
(2) CHRISTOPHER STEELE

Defendants

DEFENCE

For the Forgotten Americans

STATEMENT OF TRUTH

The Defendants believe that the facts set out in these Particulars of Claim are true.

Signed:

Christopher Steele

Position: Director, Orbis Business Intelligence Ltd

Date: 03 April 2017

Simpson was asked about Steele's "Statement of Truth":

- "No copies of the pre-election memoranda were ever shown or provided to any journalist by or with the authorization of the Defendants (STEELE and ORBIS)".

- "The Defendants did not however provide any of the pre-election memoranda to any of the media or journalists, nor did they authorize anyone to do so"

- "gave off the record briefings to a small number of journalists about the pre-election memoranda in late summer/autumn 2016"

- "[t]he briefings involved the disclosure of **limited intelligence** regarding indications of Russian interference in the US election process and the possible co-ordination of members of Trump's campaign's team and Russian government officials"

- "*The New York Times, The Washington Post, Yahoo News, The New Yorker*, and CNN" were "briefed at the end of September 2016 by [Steele] and Fusion at Fusion's instruction."

- Steele "subsequently participated in further meetings at Fusion's instruction with Fusion and *New York Times, The Washington Post, and Yahoo News,* which took place mid-October 2016. *In each of those cases the briefing was conducted verbally in person.*

- "…and again at Fusion's instruction, in late October 2016 the Second Defendant briefed a journalist from Mother Jones by Skype"

FOSTER: So did you ever share either the memos or the content of the memos with the media independently of him without having discussed it with him?

SIMPSON: I think what I said was **I had spoken with reporters <u>over the course of the summer</u> and through the fall** about the investigations by the government and the controversy over connections between -- alleged connections between the Trump campaign and the Russians. Some of what we discussed was informed by Chris's reporting.

Given those media briefings, the press never published The Steele Dossier. Then, on 10 January 2017, *Buzzfeed* posted all of the memoranda. That came just a few short hours after CNN reported that "a two-page synopsis" of The Steele Dossier was provided to then-President Obama and President-elect Trump.

It's been reported that many media organizations refused to publish The Steele Dossier without "a hook". And, after being informed about FBI Director Comey's briefing at Trump Tower, CNN had that hook and went live. Here's a brief timeline:

- **06 JAN 2017. 9:44 am: FBI Chief of Staff Rybicki sends email:** *the director is coming into HQ briefly now for an update from the sensitive matter team.*

- **06 JAN 2017: Comey meets with Trump.**

- **06 JAN 2017: Comey sends email to FBI Leadership:** *I said there was something that Clapper (DNI Director) wanted me to speak to PE (President-elect Trump) alone or in a very small group. I then executed the session as planned...I said media like CNN had them (the dossier memos) and were looking for a news hook".*

- **08 JAN 2017. 12:08 pm: Deputy Director McCabe sends email:** *CNN is close to going forward with the sensitive story...the trigger for is they know the material was discussed in the brief.*

For the Forgotten Americans

BUZZFEED OWNER, BEN SMITH, EMAIL TO HIS STAFF STATES THE DOSSIER "WAS IN WIDE CIRCULATION" IN DC CIRCLES:

Ben Smith <ben@buzzfeed.com>   7:25 PM (6 minutes ago)
to news, Purple, Headsup

As you have probably seen, this evening we published a secret dossier making explosive and unverified allegations about Donald Trump and Russia. I wanted to briefly explain to you how we made the decision to publish it.

We published the dossier, which Ken Bensinger obtained through his characteristically ferocious reporting, so that, as we wrote, "Americans can make up their own minds about allegations about the president-elect that have circulated at the highest levels of the US government."

Our presumption is to be transparent in our journalism and to share what we have with our readers. We have always erred on the side of publishing. In this case, the document was in wide circulation at the highest levels of American government and media. It seems to lie behind a set of vague allegations from the Senate Majority Leader to the director of the FBI and a report that intelligence agencies have delivered to the president and president-elect.

As we noted in our story, there is serious reason to doubt the allegations. We have been chasing specific claims in this document for weeks, and will continue to.

AFTER BUZZFEED, THE MEDIA WENT ON A FEEDING FRENZY:

From Russia with Love

EXPLOSIVE REPORT CLAIMS RUSSIA HAS "COMPROMISING PERSONAL AND FINANCIAL INFORMATION" ABOUT TRUMP

The full 35-page dossier details graphic, unconfirmed allegations involving the president-elect.

 BY ABIGAIL TRACY
JANUARY 10, 2017 7:81 PM   **VANITY FAIR**

National Security

Intelligence chiefs briefed Trump and Obama on unconfirmed claims Russia has compromising information on president-elect

The Washington Post
Democracy Dies in Darkness

By Greg Miller, Rosalind S. Helderman, Tom Hamburger and Steven Mufson January 10, 2017

The New York Times *Trump Received Unsubstantiated Report That Russia Had Damaging Information About Him*

By Scott Shane, Adam Goldman and Matthew Rosenberg

Jan. 10, 2017

Intel chiefs presented Trump with claims of Russian efforts to compromise him

By Evan Perez, Jim Sciutto, Jake Tapper and Carl Bernstein, CNN
Updated 5:26 PM ET, Thu January 12, 2017

 politics

UNDER OATH ANSWERS FROM: * CIA * FBI * DOJ *

There's no question that this solidified Donald Trump's dislike for CNN and, moreover, when President Trump found out how Comey provided the hook, Comey's days as Director of the FBI were numbered. Comey was fired 120 days later.

CNN has been the focus of President's Trump's media ire, yet they find themselves unscathed from the story. On the other hand, *Buzzfeed* and owner Ben Smith find themselves as a Defendant in America and "Across the Pond" in THE HIGH COURT OF JUSTICE Case: CR-2017-664.

But Buzzfeed is not going down without a fight.

On 03 August 2018, a U.S. District Judge granted *BuzzFeed's* discovery request to force federal intelligence officials to answer questions about whether they vetted The Steele Dossier in their Florida libel case: *Gubarev v. BuzzFeed* 17-cv-60246.

Meanwhile, as *Buzzfeed* fights their court battles, former DNI Director Clapper has become a rather vocal CNN analyst.

But, who gave The Steele Dossier to *Buzzfeed*?

Both Simpson and Steele have given under oath testimony denying that they gave the document to *Buzzfeed*.

QUIGLEY (D-IL): The dossier was published...What wasn't published? Are there still documents?

SIMPSON: Well, to just put it on the record, we were not the ones that gave this document to *Buzzfeed*, and I was not happy when this was published. I was very upset. I thought it was a very dangerous thing and that someone had violated my confidences, in any event. I think the story is largely known and that there's very little that was left on the cutting room table from that time.

HPSCI REDACTED PERSON: Do you know who did provide the dossier to *Buzzfeed*?

SIMPSON: No. I have my suspicions, but they are just guesses.

"I read a lot of books and studies on Russia and organized crime."

"I collect, you know, research on various people who are oligarchs or mafia figures."

"You know, in the background of **<u>ALL</u>** international business is questions about corruption."

Glenn R. Simpson – Founder & CEO Fusion GPS

THE FBI & HOW IT ALL STARTED

"He (Steele) said don't worry about that, I know the perfect person, I have a contact there, they'll listen to me, they know who I am, I'll take care of it."

In answering the questions by Heather Sawyer, Chief Oversight Counsel for Senator Feinstein (D-CA), Simpson says:

Q: Okay. So let me just stop you there and let's just make sure we get the sequencing accurate.

A: Sure.

Q: So after Mr. Steele had found out the information that he put in the very first of these memos, the one dated June 20, 2016, he approached you about taking this information to specifically the FBI?

A: That's my recollection.

Q: So to the best of your recollection, that request or idea came directly from Mr. Steele, not anyone else?

A: That's right.

Q: And who was involved in discussions about whether it was appropriate to take either the memo or the information in the memo to the FBI?

A: It was Chris and me. I mean, that's the only ones I remember, the two of us. The only ones I know of.

Q: And do you recall when you and Mr. Steele decided that he could or should take this to the FBI approximately the time frame of that?

A: I believe it was sometime around the turn of the month. It would have been in late June or at latest early July. That's my recollection... This was -- to me this was like, you know, you're driving to work and you see something happen and you call 911, right. Like if you're a lawyer and, you know, you find out about a crime, in a lot of countries you must report that.

So it was like that. So I just said if that's your obligation, then you (Steele) should fulfill your obligation.

What was so astonishing that Simpson and Steele felt so obligated, like a 911 call, to inform the FBI? Simpson says that it was the First Memo, often referred to as "The Pee Tape", below:

===

COMPANY INTELLIGENCE REPORT 2016/080

US PRESIDENTIAL ELECTION: REPUBLICAN CANDIDATE DONALD TRUMP'S ACTIVITIES IN RUSSIA AND COMPROMISING RELATIONSHIP WITH THE KREMLIN

Summary

- Russian regime has been cultivating, supporting and assisting TRUMP for at least 5 years. Aim, endorsed by PUTIN, has been to encourage splits and divisions in western alliance
- So far TRUMP has declined various sweetener real estate business deals offered him in Russia in order to further the Kremlin's cultivation of him. However he and his inner circle have accepted a regular flow of intelligence from the Kremlin, including on his Democratic and other political rivals
- Former top Russian intelligence officer claims FSB has compromised TRUMP through his activities in Moscow sufficiently to be able to blackmail him. According to several knowledgeable sources, his conduct in Moscow has included perverted sexual acts which have been arranged/ monitored by the FSB
- A dossier of compromising material on Hillary CLINTON has been collated by the Russian intelligence Services over many years and mainly comprises bugged conversations she had on various visits to Russia and intercepted phone calls rather than any embarrassing conduct. The dossier is controlled by Kremlin spokesman, PESKOV,

directly on orders. However it has not as yet been distributed abroad, including to TRUMP. Russian intentions for its deployment still unclear

Detail

1. Speaking to a trusted compatriot in June 2016 sources A and B, a senior Russian Foreign Ministry figure and a former top level Russian intelligence officer still active inside the Kremlin respectively, the Russian authorities had been cultivating and supporting US Republican presidential candidate, Donald TRUMP for at least 5 years. Source B asserted that the TRUMP operation was both supported and directed by Russian President Vladimir PUTIN. Its aim was to sow discord and disunity both within the US itself, but more especially within the Transatlantic alliance which was Viewed as inimical to Russia's interests. Source C, a senior Russian financial official said the TRUMP operation should be seen in terms of PUTIN's desire to return to Nineteenth Century "Great Power" politics anchored upon countries' interests rather than the ideals-based international order established after World War Two. S/he had overheard talking in way to close associates on several occasions.

2. In terms of specifics, **Source A confided that the Kremlin had been feeding TRUMP and his team valuable intelligence on his opponents, including Democratic presidential candidate Hillary CLINTON, for several years** [see more below]. This was confirmed by Source D, a close associate of TRUMP who had organized and managed his recent trips to Moscow, and who reported, also in June 2016, that this Russian intelligence had been "very helpful". **The Kremlin's cultivation operation on TRUMP also had comprised offering him various lucrative real estate development business deals in Russia,** especially in relation to the ongoing 2018 World Cup soccer tournament, However, so far, **for reasons unknown, TRUMP had not taken up any of these.**

3. However, there were other aspects to TRUMP's engagement with the Russian authorities. **One which had borne fruit for them was to exploit personal obsessions and sexual perversion in order to obtain suitable "kompromat"** [compromising material] on him. According to Source D, where s/he had been present, (perverted) conduct in Moscow included hiring the presidential suite of the Ritz Carlton Hotel, **where he knew President and OBAMA [whom he**

hated] had stayed on one other official trips to Russia, and defiling the bed where they had slept by employing a number of prostitutes to perform a 'golden showers' (urination) show in front of him. The hotel was known to be under FSB control with microphones and concealed cameras in all the main rooms to record anything they wanted to.

4. The Moscow Ritz Carlton episode involving TRUMP reported above was confirmed by Source E READACTED who said that s/he and several of the staff were aware and subsequently. S/he believed it had happened in 2013. Source E provided an introduction for a company ethnic Russian operative to Source F, a female staffer at the hotel when TRUMP had stayed there, who also confirmed the story. Speaking separately in June 2016, Source B [the former top level Russian intelligence officer) asserted that unorthodox behavior in Russia over the years had provided **the authorities there with enough embarrassing material on the now Republican presidential candidate to be able to blackmail him if they so wished**.

5. Asked about the Kremlin's reported intelligence feed to TRUMP over recent years and rumours about a Russian dossier of "kompromat" on Hillary CLINTON (being circulated), Source B confirmed the file's existence. S/he confided in a trusted compatriot that it had been collated by Department K of the FSB for many years, dating back to her husband Bill's presidency, and comprised mainly eavesdropped conversations of various sorts rather than details/evidence of unorthodox or embarrassing behavior. Some of the conversations were from bugged comments CLINTON had made on her various trips to Russia and focused on things she had said which contradicted her current position on various issues. Others were most probably from phone intercepts.

6. Continuing on this theme, Source G, a senior Kremlin official, confided that the CLINTON dossier was controlled exclusively by chief spokesman, Dmitriy PESKOV, who was responsible for compiling/handling it on the explicit instructions of PUTIN himself. The dossier however had not as yet been made available abroad, including to TRUMP or his campaign team. At present it was unclear what intentions were in this regard.

20 June 2016

==

That's it! The entire memo, as written by Steele, that started everything – the actual reason for Steele going to the FBI.

And Simpson stuck by Steele's memos. Ms. Sawyer gave him chances to move away from The Steele Dossier, but he did not.

Q: Did you have any input or involvement in the drafting of these or input for the research?

A: No.

Q: And did you edit any of them in any way?

A: No.

Q: So these were documents (memos comprising Steele Dossier) that you were just receiving from Mr. Steele?

A: Yes. I mean, the only qualifier I'd add is I'm sure I said things like Paul Manafort was just named campaign manager, what do you know about him, that kind of thing.

For nearly two years, the mainstream media has informed Americans how Russian Intelligence promotes disinformation. How they lie. How they start controversies. Well. . .?

Personally, I have no doubt that Putin wants to see the downfall of America. But, if that's the case, why wouldn't he release the Trump video in the Moscow Ritz Carlton? Think about it. As a multi-billionaire, Putin doesn't need the money. He wants the U.S. sanctions stopped, America out of Iran and Syria, the United States to stop shipping weapons to the Ukraine, etc.

"All 17 Intelligence Agencies" have told us how Putin wants "to sow discord and disunity" in America. Correct?

If publically presented, "The Pee Tape" would do just that.

The video's unveiling would certainly lead to immediate impeachment proceedings of President Trump. The country would be in complete turmoil. Russia would be elated, and Putin's objective to disgrace the United States would be done.

"*The FBI does not* believe that [Steele] directly provided this information to the press" (emphasis added)."

Chairman Grassley and Senator Graham.

"On November 1, 2016... FBI handling agent advised that CHS (Steele) was not to operate to obtain any intelligence whatsoever on behalf of the FBI."

THE FBI

THE FBI & STEELE

"That he (Steele) broke off, which implies that he told him he didn't want to have anything more to do with them (FBI)."

That's what Glenn Simpson said to Ranking Member Feinstein's Chief Oversight Counsel, Heather Sawyer.

In reading hundreds of pages where Simpson praises Steele as a trusted former MI6 Crown Servant, one would assume that: Steele is honest. Steele is reliable. Steele is credible.

For example, on the severing of the FBI-Steele relationship, Simpson testified at the August 2017 Senate Examination:

*I understand **Chris severed his relationship** with the FBI out of concern that he didn't know what was happening inside the FBI and there was a concern that the FBI was being manipulated for political ends by the Trump people and that we didn't really understand what was going on. So he stopped dealing with them.*

Simpson also stated that he wasn't aware that Steele was working for the FBI and on their payroll:

Well, we learned -- sometime after the election we learned that Chris had discussed working for the FBI on these matters after the election and that that didn't happen.

SAWYER: And I think you've already answered this question, but to the best of your knowledge, **did Mr. Steele ever obtain payment from the FBI** for actual research that he was doing on Russian interference or on possible ties between the Trump campaign and Russia?

SIMPSON: **He told me he did not**, and I have no independent information other than what he told me. I don't believe he ever received compensation for working on anything related to Trump and Russia.

I don't have any reason to believe that he (Steele) did anything that I didn't authorize or approve...He's basically a Boy Scout.

He repeated the "Boy Scout" description of Steele during the November HPSCI Hearing:

I think I might have said somewhere else that he was a Boy Scout. And, you know, he's just a fairly buttoned-down kind of guy who you could count on to do the work.

As it turns out, Steele had been on the FBI payroll for quite some time. Also, it was the FBI that severed their relationship by terminating his status as a Confidential Human Resource (CHS).

On 03 August 2018, a 72-page FBI document – provided in the *Judicial Watch v. DOJ* (No. 1:17-cv-00916) response to the FOIA request "for records of communication and payments between the FBI and Steele" – revealed that there were:

1. Fifteen (15) FD-1023 - FBI Source Reports.*
2. Thirteen (13) FD-209a - FBI Contact Reports.*
3. Eleven (11) FD-794b - FBI Payment Requests.*

CHS confirmed to an outside third party that CHS has a confidential relationship with the FBI. CHS was used as a source for an online article. In the article, CHS revealed CHS' relationship with the FBI as well as information that CHS obtained and provided to FBI.

On November 1, 2016, CHS confirmed all of this to the handling agent. At that time, handling agent advised CHS that the nature of the relationship between the FBI and CHS would change completely and that it was unlikely that the FBI would continue a relationship with the CHS.

"Additionally, (FBI) handling agent advised that CHS (Steele) was not to operate to obtain any intelligence whatsoever on behalf of the FBI."

WHO'S THE "BOY SCOUT"?

While Steele was getting paid by Fusion, he was also getting paid by the FBI. We, in America, call that "Double Dipping".

*** Steele was also a paid FBI source for non-related work.**

My father, a former US Marine and decorated Detroit Police Officer, also boxed. One of the first things he taught me as a young lad was: *The reason they call it a "sucker punch" is because you're the sucker that got hit!*

And, by the way, the "buttoned-down Boy Scout" is being sued in London for libelous statements in his dossier and, in America, Steele was criminally referred to Deputy AG Rod Rosenstein. The Grassley-Graham Memo states:

> But there is substantial evidence suggesting that Mr. Steele materially misled the FBI about a key aspect of **his dossier** efforts, one which bears on his credibility.

> **"Accordingly, we are referring Christopher Steele to the Department of Justice for investigation of potential violation(s) of 18 U.S.C. § 1001."**

MORE AT THE HPSCI HEARING BY REDACTED PERSON:

Q: So in early July, is it fair to say in early July that you knew that Mr. Steele had taken some information to the FBI?

A: I think he said he was going to, and then later he told me he did.

Q: When did that occur, approximately?

A: I think it was probably right after the 4th of July.

Q: Okay. So not like a month later?

A: No.

Q: Okay. Did he (Steele) tell you about any other communications he had with the FBI in relation to this matter?

A: Yes. -- he told me: I met with them and I informed them of my concerns...it didn't come up again for, you know, weeks if not months.

Q: Do you know if he, Mr. Steele, informed the FBI about your relationship, that is, the relationship he had with you and Fusion GPS?

A: I don't -- my recollection is that he disclosed that he was doing this for a private client, and that **he would have disclosed something about who the private client was**. I also don't think, though, that Chris at this time knew the identity of the client. And so initially, at least, he **(Steele) would have been only able to say (to the FBI): I have a political client, a Democratic client** or something like that, which is what I would have told him. So I don't think he was in a position to disclose the identity of the client to the FBI <u>originally</u>.

Q: Did the FBI ever reach out to you or Fusion GPS in relation to the matters that Mr. Steele informed them upon?

A: No.

<u>SIMPSON SAYS: STEELE MET FBI IN ROME [Senate Exam]</u>

SAWYER: So can you explain the next incident where you know that Mr. Steele met with the FBI?

SIMPSON: Yes. ... It was September (2016)...**Chris had delivered a lot of information (to the FBI)** and by this time we had, you know, stood up a good bit of it....

So anyway, we were working on all of that and then he (Steele) said, hey, I heard back from the FBI and they want me to come talk to them and they said they want everything I have, to which I said okay.

He said he had to go to Rome, I said okay. He went to Rome.

Then afterwards **he (Steele) came back (from Rome) and said, you know, I gave them (FBI) a full briefing.**

Q: Before we get to that, which I do want to hear, I just want to get a sense of the chronology.

A: Sure.

Q: So when he did that -- you had said the FBI then came back and contacted Mr. Steele?

A: That's my understanding.

Q: When did that, to the best of your knowledge, take place?

A: Mid to late September.

"And Putin essentially took over the Russian Jewish community and the leadership of the Russian Jewish community."

"The Orthodox church is also an arm of the Russian State now."

"You know, the Kushner's are ethnic Russian and they, we were told, had relationships of their own with Russian capital."

Glenn R. Simpson – Founder & CEO, Fusion GPS

Case 0:18-mc-60528-UU Document 50 Entered on FLSD Docket 07/26/2018 Page 1 of 16

UNITED STATES DISTRICT COURT
SOUTHERN DISTRICT OF FLORIDA

In re Third Party Subpoena to Fusion GPS   Case No. 18-mc-60528 (UU)

_____/

ALEKSEJ GUBAREV, XBT HOLDING S.A.,
AND WEBZILLA, INC.,
                              Plaintiffs,   Case No. 17-cv-60426 (UU)

vs.

BUZZFEED, INC. AND BEN SMITH,

                              Defendants.

_____/

Case 1:17-cv-02041-RJL Document 17 Filed 12/12/17 Page 1 of 18

UNITED STATES DISTRICT COURT
DISTRICT OF COLUMBIA
---X

MIKHAIL FRIDMAN, PETR AVEN, AND   :
GERMAN KHAN,   :   Case 1:17-cv-02041 (RJL)
                    Plaintiffs,   :

        -v-   :

BEAN LLC (A/K/A FUSION GPS) AND   :
GLENN SIMPSON,   :
                                     :
                                     :
                    Defendants.   :
---X

AMENDED COMPLAINT
JURY TRIAL DEMANDED

IN THE SUPERIOR COURT OF THE DISTRICT OF COLUMBIA

CIVIL DIVISION

---X
                                     :
MIKHAIL FRIDMAN, PETR AVEN, AND   :
GERMAN KHAN,   :   **18-0002667**
  c/o CARTER LEDYARD & MILBURN LLP   :   2018 CA _____
  2 Wall Street   :
  New York, NY 10005,   :
                                     :   **COMPLAINT**
                    Plaintiffs,   :

        -v-   :
                                     :
ORBIS BUSINESS INTELLIGENCE LIMITED :
AND CHRISTOPHER STEELE,   :
  9-11 Grosvenor Gardens   :
  London SW1W OBD.   :
                                     :
                    Defendants.   :
---X

FACT v. ALLEGATION

ALLEGATION – an assertion unsupported and by implication regarded as unsupportable.

It's a <u>fact</u> that The Steele Dossier raw intelligence. It's a <u>fact</u> that Christopher Steele has had his credibility called into question by the Plaintiffs in a London libel suit and in a Florida defamation suit. It's a <u>fact</u> that U.S. Senators have referred Steele for a criminal investigation. It's a <u>fact</u> that The Steele Dossier was used for FISA Warrants. It's a <u>fact</u> that Steele went to the press.

What is a fact? Well, depending on the dictionary employed – Oxford, Mirriam-Webster, Cambridge, Law etc. – definitions can, somewhat, vary. However, since the former British MI6 Agent is a Cambridge graduate and given the <u>fact</u> that he authored the Dossier, let's use two prominent U.K. Dictionaries.

<u>As Defined by the Oxford English Dictionary</u>:

FACT: A thing that is known or proved to be true.

FACTS: Information used as evidence or as part of a report or news article. *Law:* The truth about events as opposed to interpretation.

<u>As Defined by the Cambridge Dictionary</u>:

ALLEGATION: A statement, made without giving proof, that someone has done something wrong or illegal:

What's the purpose of this remedial exercise? It has to do with the information in The Steele Dossier: why it's included, where it came from, and motives behind said information.

Congressman Trey Gowdy (R-SC), a former US Attorney who has prosecuted numerous cases, asked Glenn Simpson the difference between the two in his opening questioning at the November HPSCI Hearing. And, here's how it went:

HPSCI HEARING – November 14, 2017 – Simpson under oath.

GOWDY: "All right. Let me ask you about a couple words you just used. You just used the words "good" and "bad," which some would argue are inherently subjective; but you also used the word "facts," and what did you mean when you used the word "facts"?"

SIMPSON: "I mean, factual information is - a lot of what we do is gather facts. And sometimes facts are provable facts; sometimes facts are established facts; sometimes they're allegations, factual allegations. So we do all of the above."

"When you gather up lawsuit information, for example, you have two sides making factual allegations against each other; and what's important is that you have a reliable, credible basis for your information. "

"And, you know, it is a lot like journalism in that journalism is called the first draft of history, where essentially you're gathering up information, and **your job is not to determine the truth**, it's to gather credible information and to present all the possibilities and all the reliable information you can find."

"But, you know, every day in the newspaper every story has two sides to it, and it's not the reporter's job to figure out who's telling the truth and who's not or who's right and who's wrong, it's to be responsible and professional in gathering up all of the facts and allegations and presenting them in a neutral way. So our method is journalistic, and our reports are written along those lines."

GOWDY: "Do you draw a distinction between facts and allegations?"

SIMPSON: "Certainly".

GOWDY: "What is that distinction?"

SIMPSON: "Well, I mean, a fact is something that's subjectively verifiable to all reasonable observers; and an allegation is something that hasn't been confirmed."

How can a fact be "something that's <u>subjectively verifiable</u> to all reasonable observers"? Our Mirriam-Webster Dictionary states: Fact – "is a piece of information presented as having **objective** reality". And, how can something be subjective to **all**? Subjectively is defined as "pertaining to or characteristic of an individual; personal; individual".

BELOW ARE SOME ALLEGATIONS THAT SIMPSON MADE:

- And Putin essentially took over the Russian Jewish community and the leadership of the Russian Jewish community.

- **The Orthodox church is also an arm of the Russian State now.**

- You know, **the Kushners are ethnic Russian** and they, we were told, had relationships of their own with Russian capital.

- I believe that he's (Trump) been to Russia a minimum of four or five times, and that he's been going to Russia since late Soviet years.

- We also had sort of more broadly learned that Mr. Trump had long time associations with Italian organized crime figures.

- It seemed as if during the early part of his career he (Trump) had connections to a lot of **Italian mafia figures**, and then gradually during the nineties became associated with **Russian mafia figures**.

- Beginning in the mid-2000s he (Trump) was not a creditworthy businessman. And so he - you know, so if you're analyzing, you know, someone who says they're a billionaire but can't get a bank loan, you know, there's this whole issue of where is the credit coming from. And so, you know, we were always trying to figure out where - how he was financing various things.

- We saw indications that some of the (Trump) money came from Kazakhstan, among other places, and that some of it you just couldn't account for.

- We looked at the golf courses and whether they actually ever made any money and how much debt they had... And these golf courses

For the Forgotten Americans

(Scotland and Ireland) are just, you know, they're sinks. They don't actually make any money.

- We heard from people familiar with the story was that the Kushner family and their connections were a big attraction for Trump before the marriage and that, you know -- I mean, I don't want to -- I'm trying to be polite about it, but, I mean, there was a business element to the whole, you know, connection.

- In the Refusenik era, there was a lot of **Russian Jewish immigration to the New York area. And a lot of those people...became very successful and wealthy**. And, as I understand it, those are the connections that the Kushners have to outside capital.

- I don't know if you have ever asked Ivanka Trump what she was doing in Kazakhstan, but she was there. So was Don Jr., I believe. She talks about it in her book. She doesn't say what she was doing there, you but she says she was there. I think she mentions eating a cow stomach.

- Donald Trump Jr. was - had done a lot of travel to Russia and was involved in a lot of these discussions that he'd done -- he'd gone to Kazakhstan for reasons that we didn't - we weren't sure of, he'd gone to Latvia, and he'd been to Russia. And we eventually formed the view that the Russians were very interested in him or that he'd had a lot of deals with them. I don't remember a lot of specifics beyond that.

"Basically because everyone in Russia, you know, more or less works for the government... I'm not saying they did anything illegal."

"Well, the facts are beyond what's here. I don't have any additional facts...I mean, it's probably in here somewhere."

Glenn R. Simpson – Founder & CEO Fusion GPS

VERIFICATION

"Generally speaking, most of this information is useful for making decisions and trying to understand what's going on, but -- doesn't have much use beyond that unless you can independently verify it."

That was Simpson's response to a question by Chief Oversight Counsel for Ranking Member Diane Feinstein (D-CA), Heather Sawyer. During the 8-hour examination, Ms. Sawyer delved into The Steele Dossier details and dissected each memo with Simpson for verification.

And, as a lawyer, she didn't bother with political biases. She stuck to the point! Below are examples:

Simpson's answers on verification of The Steele Dossier

Q: -- if we could just move on to kind of the next memo, which begins with Bates No. 41394 and it ends with 41396. It appears to be -- it's three pages and it has a date of 26 July 2015 and it has "Company Intelligence Report 2016/086." To the best of your recollection, was this the second memo you had received from Mr. Steele?

A: To the best of my recollection, this is the second memo.

Q: I'm going to direct your attention back to what we marked as Exhibit 3 (Steel Dossier), which is the series of memos that you had received from Mr. Steele in the course of his work.
We talked about the first memo and we also talked about the second memo to some degree.
You were explaining to me why you believed the second memo (Co. Intelligence Report 2016/86), which starts at page 41394 (page in the Senate Exam material), came about...
So with regard to that memo, were there any particular things that you independently verified?

A: I just need to review it here for a second...

(Reviewing document.)

Most of this (memo two 2016/86) I did not seek to independently verify and was relatively new information.

===

STEELE DOSSIER MEMO TWO (excerpts)

COMPANY INTELLIGENCE REPORT 2016/086
RUSSIA/CYBER CRIME: A SYNOPSIS OF RUSSIAN STATE SPONSORED AND OTHER CYBER OFFENSIVE (CRIMINAL) OPERATIONS

Summary:

- Russia has extensive programme of state-sponsored offensive cyber operations...using corporate and other visitors to Russia.
- FSB often uses coercion and **blackmail** to recruit most capable cyber operatives in Russia into its state sponsored programmes. Heavy use also, both wittingly and unwittingly, of CIS emigres working in western corporations and ethnic Russians employed by neighbouring governments e.g. Latvia.
- Example cited of successful Russian cyber operation targeting senior Western business visitor...
- Example given of US citizen of Russian origin approached by FSB and offered incentive of "investment" in his business when visiting Moscow.
- Problems however for Russian authorities themselves in countering local hackers and cyber criminals, operating outside state control...
- Some details given of leading non-state Russian cyber criminal groups

Detail (excerpts):

2. In terms of the FSB's recruitment of capable cyber operatives to carry out its, ideally deniable, offensive cyber operations, a Russian IT specialist with direct knowledge reported in June 2016 that this was often done using coercion and blackmail. In terms of 'foreign' agents, **the FSB was approaching US citizens of Russian Jewish origin on business trips to Russia.**

26 July 2016

===

MS. SAWYER continues:

Q: And how did you kind of use this information?

A: Well, I think the context of external events is important here. I believe -- it's my recollection that what prompted this memo was, in fact, the beginning of public reporting on the hack. I think -- what is the date again? Yeah, it's 26 July. And I think this is also -- by the time this memo was written (26 July 2016) Chris had already met with the FBI about the first memo (20 June 2016).

He (Steele) thought from his perspective there was an issue -- a security issue about whether a presidential candidate (Trump) was being **blackmailed.**

From my perspective there was a law enforcement issue about whether there was an illegal conspiracy to violate the campaign laws, and then somewhere in this time the whole issue of hacking has also surfaced. So he proposed to -- he said we should tell the FBI, it's a national security issue.

In any event, he (Steele) said don't worry about that, I know the perfect person, I have a contact there, they'll listen to me, they know who I am, I'll take care of it.

Q: You said you had asked for some time to think it over. What in particular did he articulate to you was of significant national security concern to indicate that it should be taken to the FBI?

A: His (Steele's) concern, which is something that counterintelligence people deal with a lot, is whether or not there was blackmail going on, whether a political candidate (Trump) was being blackmailed or had been compromised...

So, you know, a trained intelligence officer can spot disinformation that you or I might not recognize, certainly that was Chris's skill, and he honed in on this issue of blackmail as being a significant national security issue. Chris is the professional and I'm not.

So I didn't agree with that -- it wasn't that I disagreed with it. It was that I didn't feel qualified to be the arbitrar of whether this is a national security expert. He's the pro and I'm the ex-journalist.

Q: And with specific regard to the issue of BLACKMAIL, what was the -- what were the FACTS that he (Steele) had gathered that made him concerned about the possibility of blackmail and who did he think was going to be blackmailed?

A: Well, the facts are beyond what's here I don't have any additional facts. The alleged incident that's described here is the one that he was referring to. As I say, I don't have really any additional information beyond this except that -- I mean, it's probably in here somewhere actually, but it's well known in intelligence circles that the Russians have cameras in all the luxury hotel rooms and there are memoirs written about this by former Russian intelligence agents I could quote.

NEXT MEMO ANALYZED

Q: Then similarly with what I have -- and I'm just doing it in the order that it was Bates-stamped and appeared on *BuzzFeed* -- there's a two-page report and it bears the Bates Nos. 41397 and 41398 and it has a company report number 2016/095...

It does not bear a date on it. Do you recall roughly when you received this particular report?

A: Sometime in midsummer.

==

STEELE DOSSIER MEMO THREE (excerpts)

COMPANY INTELLIGENCE REPORT 2016/095
RUSSIA/US PRESIDENTIAL ELECTION: FURTHER INDICATIONS OF EXTENSIVE CONSPIRACY BETWEEN TRUMP'S CAMPAIGN TEAM AND THE KREMLIN
Summary:

- Further evidence of extensive conspiracy between TRUMP's campaign team and Kremlin, sanctioned at highest levels and involving Russian diplomatic staff based in the US
- TRUMP associate admits Kremlin behind recent appearance of DNC e-mails on WikiLeaks, as means of maintaining plausible deniability

- Agreed exchange of information established in both directions. **TRUMPS team using moles within DNC and hackers** in the US as well as outside in Russia. PUTIN motivated by fear and hatred of Hillary CLINTON. Russians receiving intel from TRUMP's team on Russian oligarchs and their families in US
- Mechanism for transmitting this intelligence involves **"pension" disbursements to Russian emigres living in US as cover**, using consular officials in New York, DC and Miami
- Suggestion from source close to TRUMP and MANAFORT that Republican campaign team happy to have Russia as media bogeyman to mask more extensive corrupt business ties to China and other emerging countries

Detail:

1. Speaking in confidence to a compatriot in late July 2016, Source E, an ethnic Russian **close associate of Republican US presidential candidate Donald TRUMP, admitted that there was a well-developed conspiracy of co-operation between them and the Russian leadership.** This was managed on the TRUMP side by the Republican candidate's campaign manager, Paul MANAFORT, who was using foreign policy advisor, Carter PAGE, and others as intermediaries....

==

Q: And then just in general, with regard to this particular memo did you do any research to verify this information that was in this memo? Was there particular information in this memo that you did verify?

A: One of the things I did, which is pretty typical of how I would sort of analyze things, was I looked at the Russian pension system to determine if, in fact, the Russian government was distributing lots of pension payments to Russian immigrants in the United States, and I found some reports from the Social Security Administration and other places describing this system.

Basically because everyone in Russia, you know, more or less works for the government, there's a lot of – there's a large number of Russian emigres in the United States who receive pension payments that are paid through the embassies and various people, Russian lawyers and others who we became interested in in the course of this investigation seem to be involved in that process.

I'm not saying they did anything illegal. I'm just saying, you know, we looked at this system, and as someone who does a lot of money laundering work this was an interesting thing that I hadn't heard about. There's all this money flowing in the United States from Russia, it probably flows in under some sort of diplomatic status...

Q: And in answering that you said that some of the officials that you had identified as involved in this effort seemed to come up with regard to the pension disbursements. Who specifically are you referring to?

A: We identified a lawyer in Sunny Isles Beach, Florida who said she previously worked for Gazprom and just had on her professional Website or someplace that she was -- she had some kind of relationship with the Russian embassy in dealing with these pension issues.

Q: And do you recall that lawyer's name?

A: I don't.

NEXT MEMO ANALYZED

Q: ...a two-page document, 41399 to 41400, and it has the date, I think you indicated before, 19 July 2016. Is this the memo (memo four 2016/094) that you said you referred to as the Carter Page memo?

A: Yes.

==

STEELE DOSSIER MEMO FOUR (CARTER PAGE - FULL)

COMPANY INTELLIGENCE REPORT 2016/094
RUSSIA: KREMLIN MEETINGS ATTENDED BY TRUMP ADVISOR
CARTER PAGE IN MOSCOW (JULY 2016)
Summary:
- TRUMP advisor Carter PAGE holds secret meetings in Moscow with SECHIN and senior Kremlin Internal Affairs official, DIVYEKIN
- SECHIN raises issues of future bilateral US-Russia energy co-operation and associated lifting of western sanctions against Russia over Ukraine. PAGE non-committal in response
- DIVEYKIN discusses release of Russian **dossier** of "kompromat" on TRUMP's opponent, Hillary CLINTON, but also hints at Kremlin possession of such material on TRUMP

1. Speaking in July 2016, a Russian source close to Rosneft President, PUTIN close associate and US-sanctioned individual, Igor SECHIN, confided the details of a recent secret meeting between him and visiting Foreign Affairs Advisor to Republican presidential candidate Donald TRUMP, Carter PAGE.

2. According to SECHIN's associate, the Rosneft President (CEO) had raised with PAGE the issues of future bilateral energy cooperation and prospects for an associated move to lift Ukraine-related western sanctions against Russia. PAGE had reacted positively to this demarche by SECHIN but had been generally non-committal in response.

3. Speaking separately, also in July 2016, an official close to Presidential Administration Head, S. IVANOV, confided in a compatriot that a senior colleague in the Internal Political Department of the PA, DIVYEKIN (nfd) also had met secretly with PAGE on his recent visit. Their agenda had included DIVEYKIN raising a **dossier** of "kompromat" the Kremlin possessed on Democratic presidential rival, Hillary CLINTON, and its possible release to the Republican's campaign team.

4. However, the Kremlin official close to S. IVANOV added that s/he believed DIVEYKIN also had hinted (or indicated more strongly) that the Russian leadership also had "kompromat" on TRUMP which the latter should bear in mind in his dealings with them.

19 July 2016

===

Sawyer continues...

Q: So with regard to the research you were also doing, is it also just true that whatever independent research you were doing did not then get incorporated into document company report 2016/94, the Carter Page memo?

A: That's correct. We essentially segregated this reporting from other things we were doing for reasons we discussed earlier. A lot of this is human intelligence, it's not the kind of thing that you would share with almost anyone basically. Generally speaking, most of this information is useful for making decisions and trying to understand what's going on, but it's not -- **doesn't have much use beyond that unless you can independently verify it.** So our reports are full of footnotes and appendices and court records and that sort of thing.

Q: So is it fair to characterize the research that you were doing as kind of a separate track of research on the same topic sometimes?

A: I think so. I wouldn't say it was completely separate because, for instance, on some subjects I knew more than Chris. ...

In British intelligence the methodology's a little different from American intelligence. There's a practice of being faithful to what people are saying.

So these are relatively straightforward recitations of things that people have said. Obviously, as we talked about, you know, disinformation is an issue that Chris wrestles with, has wrestled with his entire life. So if he believed any of this was disinformation, he would have told us.

Q: And did he ever tell you that information in any of these memos, that he had concerns that any of it was disinformation?

A: No. What he said was disinformation is an issue in my profession, that is a central concern and that we are trained to spot disinformation, and if I believed this was disinformation or I had concerns about that I would tell you that and I'm not telling you that.

I'm telling you that I don't believe this is disinformation.

Q: So beyond what is in the **dossier**, did you kind of find any evidence that he had actually been compromised? I'm speaking of Carter Page.

A: Well, the definition of compromised is someone who has been influenced sometimes without even their knowledge. We had reason to believe **that he (Page) had, in fact, been offered business deals that were -- that would tend to influence him, business arrangements**.

Q: And do you have the records of those (Page) business deals that you had collected?

A: Yeah. I don't think so. Most of that was, in fact, reporting that we did with other people who knew him from the business world.

NEXT MEMO ANALYZED

Q: Just moving on to the next memo, which is Company Intelligence Report 2016/097, it bears the Bates Nos. 401 and 41402, it's a two-page memo dated 30 July 2016.

===

STEELE DOSSIER MEMO FIVE (excerpts)

COMPANY INTELLIGENCE REPORT 2016/097

RUSSIA-US PRESIDENTIAL ELECTION: KREMLIN CONCERN THAT POLITICAL FALLOUT FROM DNC E-MAIL HACKING AFFAIR SPIRALLING OUT OF CONTROL

Summary:

- Kremlin concerned that political fallout from DNC e-mail hacking operation is spiraling out of control. Extreme nervousness among associates as result of negative media attention/accusations
- Russians meanwhile keen to cool situation and maintain "plausible deniability" of existing /ongoing and operations. Therefore unlikely to be any ratcheting up offensive plays in immediate future
- Source close to TRUMP campaign however confirms regular exchange with Kremlin has existed for at least 8 years, including intelligence fed back to Russia on oligarchs' activities in US
- Russians apparently have promised not to use "kompromat" they hold on TRUMP as leverage, given high levels of voluntary co-operation forthcoming from his team

30 July 2016 [Detail: see full memo online]

===

Q: Again, when you take a look at that, was there anything that you independently verified that comes out of this memo?

A: I don't think so.

NEXT MEMO ANALYZED

===

STEELE DOSSIER MEMO SIX (excerpts)

COMPANY INTELLIGENCE REPORT 2016/100

RUSSIA/USA: GROWING BACKLASH IN KREMLIN TO DNC HACKING AND TRUMP SUPPORT OPERATIONS

Summary:

- Head of PA IVANOV laments Russian intervention in US presidential election and black PR against CLINTON and the DNC. Vows not to supply intelligence to Kremlin PR operatives again. Advocates now sitting tight and denying everything
- Presidential spokesman PESKOV the main protagonist in Kremlin campaign to aid TRUMP and damage CLINTON. He is now scared and fears being made scapegoat by leadership for backlash in US. Problem compounded by his botched intervention in Turkish crisis
- Premier office furious over DNC hacking and associated anti-Russian publicity. Want good relations with US and ability to travel there. Refusing to support or help cover up after PESKOV
- Talk now in Kremlin of TRUMP withdrawing from presidential race altogether, but this still largely wishful thinking by more liberal elements in Moscow

5 August 2016 **[Detail:** see full memo online**]**

==

MS. SAWYER continues:

Q: Okay. Then Company Intelligence Report 2016/100, was there any information there that you either independently verified or had independent research on any of the individuals mentioned in there. It mentions Sergei Ivanov, Dmitry Peskov. What we're trying to determine is, is there information that either you had in your possession that corroborated and verified this (memo six) or even went beyond what was in this and amplified information on any of these individuals relevant to Russia's interference or possible ties with the Trump campaign?

A: Yes. I'm trying to be as helpful as I can. The thing that we worked on with regard to Sergei Ivanov, who was the head of what's called the head of administration which we confirmed from open sources is kind of an internal Kremlin intelligence operation, and that Ivanov according to experts on Russia, the Russian military, Russian intelligence, does, in fact, run this internal Kremlin intelligence operation that sort of sits atop the FSB and the SVR, the GRU, which are the other agencies specifically tasked with areas of intelligence, military for the GRU, foreign for the SVR, domestic for the FSB...

For the Forgotten Americans

In particular I remember reading a paper by a superb academic expert whose name is Mark Galeotti...So that would have given me comfort that whoever Chris is talking to they know what they're talking about.

Q: We appreciate you are walking through some of these and we understand your general practice and I want to make sure I'm characterizing this accurately. When you would get the memos you would -- from Mr. Steele you would review them, you would see if they resonated with information that you already knew and other research you may already have done.

I think you already told me that **you don't recall at the time anything jumping out at you as patently inaccurate; is that fair to say?**

A: **Yes, that's fair to say.**

Q: And I had just asked you to review and I appreciate you taking the time to review the additional memos which would just run from Bates No. 41405 to 41425 to just try to determine for the committee if research that you had been doing on the separate track on some of these topics in particular amplified the work in the **dossier**.

MR. LEVY: "amplified the work in the **dossier**," what do you mean?

MS. SAWYER: Both kind of verified and maybe gave you some additional information and insights on either the factual allegations in them or whether or not the key players identified had also engaged in either similar or related behavior on Russian interference.

BY THE WITNESS [SIMPSON]

A: I'd say that's generally right. **I read a lot of books and studies on Russia and organized crime**. So over the years I just have a lot of residual knowledge of some of the people and subjects that are covered in the memos.

Q: Okay. So nothing certainly jumped out at you and then as --

A: Nothing jumped out at me --

Q: -- as inconsistent with information that you had gained from other sources?

A: That's correct.

"Steele admitted to Ohr...
he 'was desperate that Donald
Trump not get elected and was
passionate about him not being
president'...

Bruce Ohr continued to pass along
allegations from Mr. Steele after the
FBI suspended its formal
relationship with Mr. Steele..."

Chairman Grassley – Senate Judiciary Committee.

SIMPSON & THE OHR'S

In 1983, Nellie Ohr graduated from Harvard with a degree in History and Russian Literature. In 1989, she travelled to Russia and earned her PhD in Russian History from Stanford in 1990. Around June 2016, she joined Simpson's firm, Fusion GPS, "to help our company with its research and analysis of Mr. Trump".

**IN THE UNITED STATES DISTRICT COURT
FOR THE DISTRICT OF COLUMBIA**

BEAN LLC d/b/a FUSION GPS)
        Plaintiff,)
        v.)
DEFENDANT BANK,) Civil Action 17-cv-2187-RJL
        Defendant,)
        and)
PERMANENT SELECT COMMITTEE)
ON INTELLIGENCE OF THE U.S.)
HOUSE OF REPRESENTATIVES,)
        Defendant-Intervenor.)

**DECLARATION OF GLENN R. SIMPSON IN SUPPORT OF
PLAINTIFF'S NOTICE OF ADDITIONAL RECORD EVIDENCE**

I, GLENN R. SIMPSON, hereby declare as follows:

5. The bank records reflect that Fusion contracted with Nellie Ohr, a former government official expert in Russian matters, to help our company with its research and analysis of Mr. Trump I am not aware of any other sources from which the Committee or the media could have learned of this information.

6. At my voluntary interview before HPSCI, on November 14, 2017, I disclosed that I met with Bruce Ohr, at his request, after the November 2016 election to discuss our findings regarding Russia and the election I am not aware of any other sources from which the Committee or the media could have learned of this information.

7. I declare under penalty of perjury under the laws of the United States of America that the foregoing is true and correct.

Executed on this 12th day of December 2017 in Washington, D.C.

Glenn R. Simpson

THE DOJ & BRUCE OHR

"I was asked to provide some information to the Justice Department (DOJ)."

In the 312-page Senate Exam neither Ohr nor the DOJ was mentioned. At the November HPSCI Hearing, however, Simpson stated that he gave the "DOJ's No. 4", Bruce Ohr, information:

HPSCI HEARING BY REDACTED PERSON:

Q: You've never heard from anyone in the U.S. Government in relation to those matters, either the FBI or the Department of Justice?

A: After the election. I mean, during the election, no.

Q: What did you hear after and from whom and when?

A: I was asked to provide some information to the Justice Department.

Q: By whom and when?

A: It was by a prosecutor named Bruce Ohr, who was following up. You know, I can't remember when. It was sometime after Thanksgiving, I think.

Q: Thanksgiving of 2016?

A: Yes.

Q: Did Mr. Ohr reach out to you, or how did that shake out? Originally.

A: I think Chris - it was someone that Chris Steele knows. I think--

Q: I'm sorry. Chris Steele knows who?

A: Bruce Ohr.

Q: Okay.

A: And I met Bruce too through organized crime conferences or something like that. And Chris said he had been - Chris told me that he had been talking to Bruce, that he had told Bruce about what happened, and that Bruce wanted more information, and suggested that I speak with Bruce.

For the Forgotten Americans

Today, 13 August 2018, Peter Strzok was fired from the FBI. And yesterday, the DOJ is making Bruce Ohr available for Congressional Testimony in two weeks' time on 28 AUG.

Two critical questions that need to be cleared up is

- **When did Steele inform Ohr of their Trump research and**
- **When did Simpson give information to Ohr**

Thanks to the outstanding reporting from John Solomon (*The Hill*) and Byron York (*The Washington Examiner*), America just became aware of Ohr's communications with the former MI6 Crown Servant on 05 AUG. Below is one email string.

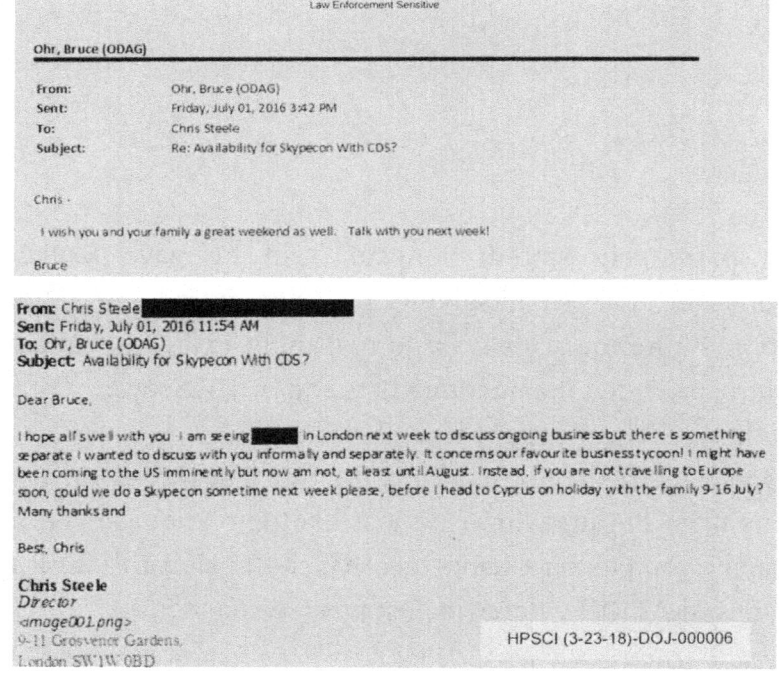

The date is 01 JULY 2016.

Steele wants "**to discuss**" his concerns with "**our favourite business tycoon**" before he leaves on holiday from 9-16 July.

But that's not all! There's more. Much more. . .

Steele met Bruce Ohr and his wife, Nellie, the morning of 30 JULY 2018 in D.C. He wants to "keep in touch on sensitive issues" and writes that "Glenn (Simpson) is happy to speak to you on this if it would help".

Chris Steele

From:	Chris Steele
Sent:	Saturday, July 30, 2016 9:36 PM
To:	Ohr, Bruce (ODAG)
Subject:	Re: CDS In DC

Great to see you and Nellie this morning Bruce. Let's keep in touch on the substantive issues/s Glenn is happy to speak to you on this if it would help.

Best, Chris

Sent from my BlackBerry 10 smartphone.
Original Message
From: Ohr, Bruce (ODAG)
Sent: Friday, 29 July 2016 22:32
To: Chris Steele
Subject: Re: CDS In DC

As previously stated, Simpson said he gave Bruce Ohr information after Thanksgiving. In other words, well after the election. Futhermore, he was, quite frankly, rather coy about Ohr and how provided the documents to the DOJ. He says:

"I think Chris...someone that Chris knows"

Moreover, he never mentions the fact that Nellie Ohr worked for his firm. Because Simpson lost his fight to quash the HPSCI subpoena for Fusion's bank records, the Fusion GPS CEP made his DECLARATION where No. 5 states (see page 55):

Fusion contracted with Nellie Ohr, a former government official expert in Russian matters, to help our company with its research and analysis of Mr. Trump.

In fact, Simpson avoided mentioning Nellie Ohr when asked by (REDACTED Person) who worked on the Trump project.

Q: Okay. Were there individuals besides yourself who either worked for Fusion or on behalf of Fusion worked on both the Prevezon project and the research for Perkins Coie?

A: I mean there is one in particular who did some work on both cases as a subcontractor. I actually think within my staff there is not much overlap. We have a long-standing relationship with a subcontractor named Ed Baumgartner who has a degree in Russian from Vassar...

Who is Ed Baumgartner? (see Page 115)

He studied Russian History at Vassar in the 1990s at the same time that Nellie Ohr taught Russian History at Vassar.

A year after Nellie Ohr graduated from Harvard, Bruce Genesoke Ohr earned his Harvard undergrad degree in physics (1984). Three years later, he obtained his law degree. And, like Nellie, he also taught college (adjunct professor at Georgetown).

Starting as a federal prosecutor in the infamous Southern District of New York (1991-99), Bruce Ohr worked his way up to "Main Justice" – the 4th floor at DOJ – and held two titles: Associate Deputy Attorney General and the Director of the Organized Crime Drug Enforcement Task Forces (OCDETF).

When Ohr began his work week on 04 December 2017, he was considered to be the No. 4 person at DOJ with an office just a few doors down from Deputy AG Rosenstein. Ohr also worked quite closely with the DOJ's Sally Yates.

By the end of the week, he was stripped of his Associate Deputy Attorney General title. And, within one month, he no longer went to work at "Main Justice" and was stripped of his OCDETF Director title.

The obvious reason why that happened: **The Steele Dossier**.

However, the HPSCI Minority Memo states that Bruce Ohr was kosher..."and **the Majority does him a grave disservice** by suggesting he is part of some malign conspiracy".

==

TO: All Members of the House of Representatives
FROM: HPSCI Minority
DATE: January 29, 2018
RE: Correcting the Record -The Russia Investigations

The HPSCI Majority's move to release to the House its allegations against the Federal Bureau of Investigation (FBI) and the Department of Justice (DOJ) is a transparent effort to undermine those agencies, the Special Counsel, and Congress' investigations. It also risks public exposure of sensitive sources and methods for no legitimate purpose.

FBI and DOJ officials did <u>not</u> "abuse" the Foreign Intelligence Surveillance Act (FISA) process, omit material information, or subvert this vital tool to spy on the Trump campaign...

- The Majority's reference to Bruce Ohr is misleading. The Majority mischaracterizes Bruce Ohr's role, overstates the significance of his interactions with Steele, and misleads about the timeframe of Ohr's communication with the FBI. In late November 2016, Ohr informed the FBI of his prior professional relationship with Steele and information that Steele shared with him (including Steele's concern about Trump being compromised by Russia). He also described his wife's contract work with Fusion GPS, the firm that hired Steele separately.

  This occurred weeks after the election and more than a month <u>after</u> the Court approved the initial FISA application. The Majority describes Bruce Ohr as a senior DOJ official who "worked closely with the Deputy Attorney General Yates and later Rosenstein," in order to imply that Ohr was somehow involved in the FISA process, but there is no indication.

- Bruce Ohr is a well-respected career professional whose portfolio is drugs and organized crime, not counterintelligence. There is no evidence that he would have known about the Page FISA applications and their contents. The Majority's assertions, moreover, are irrelevant in determining the veracity of Steele's reporting. By the time Ohr debriefs with the FBI, it had already terminated Steele as a source and was independently corroborating Steele's reporting about Page's activities. Bruce Ohr took the initiative to inform the FBI of what he knew, and **the Majority does him a grave disservice by suggesting he is part of some malign conspiracy**.

That sounds terrific. . .only if they were true!

COUNTERINTELLIGENCE: The Minority Memo states that Ohr's portfolio is "not counterintelligence." However, then-FBI Deputy Assistant Director of the Counterintelligence Division, Peter Strzok, testified that he met with Bruce Ohr. WHY?

On 12 July 2018, the FBI's Peter Strzok testified:

JORDAN: Did you communicate with Bruce Ohr?

STRZOK: Yes.

JORDAN: When did you communicate with Bruce Ohr?

STRZOK: My recollection is somewhere between three, possibly three, four or five times in late 2016, early 2017 time frame.

JORDAN: What did you talk about?

STRZOK: We talked about investigative matters that Mr. Ohr was involved in.

JORDAN: Did you talk about the investigation we're focused on here?

STRZOK: My direction from the FBI –

JORDAN: All right. All right. I got it. I got it.

STRZOK: -- may not answer that question.

STRZOK: Mr. Ohr provided information to the FBI that included material that is what everybody's calling the Dossier...he (Ohr) provided some elements of reporting that, from my understanding, originated from Mr. Steele.

JORDAN: Ohr did give the FBI information relative to the Dossier.

STRZOK: Yes.

OHR-STEELE RELATIONSHIP REVEALED: The Minority Memo claims that "The (HPSCI) Majority mischaracterizes Bruce Ohr's role, overstates the significance of his interactions with Steele, and misleads about the timeframe of Ohr's communication with the FBI", is simply false.

On 08 July 2018, Chairman Grassley wrote AG Rosenstein and FBI Director Wray:

Before and after Steele was terminated as a source, he maintained contact with DOJ via then-Associate Deputy Attorney General Bruce Ohr...Shortly after the election, the FBI began interviewing Ohr, documenting his communications with Steele.

For example, in September 2016, Steele admitted to Ohr his feelings against then-candidate Trump when

Steele said he "was desperate that Donald Trump not get elected and was passionate about him not being president."

Included in this unclassified letter were ...Numerous FD-302s demonstrating that Department of Justice official Bruce Ohr that:

- **continued to pass along allegations from Mr. Steele to the FBI after the FBI suspended its formal relationship with Mr. Steele** ...
- **and demonstrating that Mr. Ohr otherwise funneled allegations from Fusion GPS and Mr. Steele to the FBI.**

Ohr 302s:

1.	Ohr FD-302 12/19/16	(interview date 11/22/16)
2.	Ohr FD-302 12/19/16	(interview date 12/05/16)
3.	Ohr FD-302 12/19/16	(interview date 12/12/16)
4.	Ohr FD-302 12/27/16	(interview date 12/20/16)
5.	Ohr FD-302 01/27/17	(interview date 01/27/17)
6.	Ohr FD-302 01/31/17	(interview date 01/23/17)
7.	Ohr FD-302 01/27/17	(interview date 01/25/17)
8.	Ohr FD-302 02/08/17	(interview date 02/06/17)
9.	Ohr FD-302 02/15/17	(interview date 02/14/17)
10.	Ohr FD-302 05/10/17	(interview date 05/08/17)

11. Ohr FD-302 05/12/17   (interview date 05/12/17)
12. Ohr FD-302 05/16/17   (interview date 05/15/17)

As mentioned, there were literally loads of texts and emails between Ohr and Steele. The single most shocking text, thus far, was sent by Steele after he was terminated by the FBI:

Thanks...If you end up out though. I really need another (Bureau?) contact point/number who is briefed. We can't allow our guy to be forced to go back home. It would be disastrous...

OHR-STEELE ENCRYPTED TEXT REVEALED

Law Enforcement Sensitive

[1/25/17, 8:50:04 AM] ▮▮▮▮▮▮▮▮: Messages to this chat and calls are now secured with end-to-end encryption.
[1/25/17, 8:50:48 AM] Bruce: This is Bruce.
[1/25/17, 9:16:10 AM] ▮▮▮▮▮▮▮▮: Thanks. Got it. I'll call you later if I may. What time would be convenient please? Best
[1/25/17, 9:38:06 AM] Bruce: I have meetings from 1030 – 1230 my time but am otherwise free up until 1600.
[1/25/17, 12:57:13 PM] ▮▮▮▮▮▮▮▮: Missed Voice Call
[1/25/17, 12:58:06 PM] Bruce: Sorry, I just missed your call. I'm available now.
[1/25/17, 6:23:59 PM] Bruce: On Thursday I should be available most of the morning until 1200 DC time, and then again from 1330 to 1500.
[1/25/17, 6:24:57 PM] ▮▮▮▮▮▮▮▮: Noted, thanks.
[1/27/17, 9:44:23 AM] ▮▮▮▮▮▮▮▮: Hi B! Our guy's OK for the time being but I would like to keep our channel open on him and his situation if that's all right? Many thanks for your support and Best Wishes
[1/27/17, 10:38:37 AM] Bruce: Understood. We will be available if needed. Just or me know.
[1/31/17, 10:52:44 AM] ▮▮▮▮▮▮▮▮: B, doubtless a sad and crazy day for you re-SY. Just wanted to check you are OK, still in situ and able to help locally as discussed, along with your Bureau colleagues, with our guy if the need arises? Many Thanks and Best as Always, C
[1/31/17, 10:55:31 AM] Bruce: Yes, a crazy day. I'm still here and able to help as discussed. I'll let you know if that changes. Thanks!
[1/31/17, 11:12:09 AM] ▮▮▮▮▮▮▮▮: Thanks. You have my sympathy and support. If you end up out though, I really need another (Bureau?) contact point/number who is briefed. We can't allow our guy to be forced to go back home. It would be disastrous all round, though his position right now looks stable. A million thanks. C
[1/31/17, 5:48:09 PM] Bruce: Understood. I can certainly give you an FBI contact if it becomes necessary.
[2/10/17, 10:16:29 AM] ▮▮▮▮▮▮▮▮: B, Hi. Nothing dramatically new to report from here but I just wanted to check you were OK, still in place and able to stay in touch? Perhaps we could have a word on FaceTime over the weekend? Many thanks and Best as Always, C
[2/10/17, 11:07:40 AM] Bruce: Good to hear from you. I'm still here and available to chat. Happy to talk this weekend. When is a good time for you?
[2/10/17, 11:09:20 AM] ▮▮▮▮▮▮▮▮: Maybe 1000 Saturday morning your time? Or thereafter. C
[2/10/17, 11:10:40 AM] Bruce: That time is good for me. Thanks!
[3/7/17, 4:53:26 AM] ▮▮▮▮▮▮▮▮: Would it be possible to speak later today please? We're very concerned by the Grassley letter and it's possible implications for us, our operations and our sources. We need some reassurance. Many thanks
[3/7/17, 6:57:09 AM] Bruce: Sure. Would 130 today, DC time, work?
[3/7/17, 6:59:19 AM] ▮▮▮▮▮▮▮▮: Yes thanks it would. Sorry to bother you so early but I know you'll appreciate why we are concerned.

HPSCI (3-23-18)-DOJ-000025

"Did you ever obtain, with respect to the money laundering allegations, any of the President's tax returns?"

Adam Schiff (D-CA)

"No."

Glenn R. Simpson – Founder & CEO, Fusion GPS

Politics

Trump Paid $38 Million Tax on $150 Million Income, Return Shows

Bloomberg News
March 14, 2017, 9:06 PM EDT *Updated on March 15, 2017, 7:14 AM* **Bloomberg**

White House: Trump paid $38 million in income tax in 2005

By Jim Acosta, Kevin Liptak, Theodore Schleifer and Dylan Byers, CNN
Updated 11:43 AM ET, Wed March 15, 2017

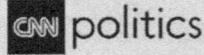 

Trump made $150 million in 2005 and paid $38 million in federal taxes

By HENRY C. JACKSON | 03/14/2017 09:42 PM EDT | Updated 03/14/2017 POLITICO

For the Forgotten Americans

A. ADAM SCHIFF. COLLUSION?

"The Washington Post" and "The New York Times" stated that Trump paid a $38 million tax bill in 2005.

At the HPSCI Hearing Ranking Member Adam Schiff (D-CA) adamantly probed Simpson for any COLLUSION relating to President Trump, the Trump Organization, and his family. Here are just a of Schiff's never-ending quest to confirm collusion:

SCHIFF: The kompromat which has become so much a focus of any discussion of the dossier, are **there any of the facts related to that, the salacious video** that were not a part of the dossier or other like allegations that came to your attention?

SIMPSON: No. I mean, you know, we were asked about other allegations by reporters that didn't come from us...

SIMPSON: The other one that is -- was concerning to us was - is the golf courses in Scotland and Ireland.

SCHIFF: Did you see Russian money involved with those as well?

SIMPSON: We saw what Eric Trump said about Russian money being available for his golf -- for the golf course projects, making remarks about having unlimited sums available...

But because the Irish courses and the Scottish courses are under U.K., you know, Anglo corporate law, they have -- they file financial statements. So we were able to get the financial statements.

And they don't, on their face, show Russian involvement, but what they do show is enormous amounts of capital flowing into these projects from unknown sources and - or at least on paper it says it's from The Trump Organization, but it's hundreds of millions of dollars.

And these golf course are just, you know, they're sinks. They don't actually make any money...

And that didn't make sense to me, doesn't make sense to this day.

SCHIFF: Did you ever obtain, with respect to the **money laundering allegations, any of the President's tax returns**?

SIMPSON: No. We did look at other ways of finding out what his practices were with regards to taxes, and we found some great, interesting documents in Las Vegas, I believe, and various other locations where he would - I think gave much more realistic assessments of the income and values of his properties.

And I suppose he would say he was lowballing them to save on taxes, but I think he was actually probably telling more truthful statements about the financial condition of a lot of his properties, which was extremely poor. So there are interesting real estate tax records among the few tax records you can get publicly.

SCHIFF: And what did you find notable about the Trump vodka issue?

SIMPSON: That it seemed like there was an orchestrated effort by someone to help Trump out with - to help him market, you know, these branded products in Russia, and that it was -- it was just very mysterious. And then we later found some of the people who came up after the first Steele memo were involved in some of those efforts.

SCHIFF: **Did Trump go to Russia on this vodka promotion** or his family members?

SIMPSON: I don't think he was there. I think his representatives were there. I don't believe there's a record of him being there himself.

SCHIFF: Mr. Simpson, just to follow up, you mentioned that one of the things that you found suspicious was that Mr. Trump would go to Russia or his son would go to Russia, and they seemed to have a great interest in Russia but never came back with any deals.

SIMPSON: Yes.

SCHIFF: And what was your suspicion what they did come back with? Are you suggesting that what they came back with was not a real estate deal but rather--Russian money that would be used in Trump properties?

SIMPSON: No, I'm not suggesting that. I mean, you know, there is my state of mind at the time and what I think now or what we eventually began to think. I honestly didn't have any preconceived notions about what was going on. I found it puzzling...

SCHIFF: And, in this case, what facts came to your attention that concerned you that the buying and selling of properties - the buying and selling of Trump properties might indicate money laundering?

SCHIFF: So if, as the President's son boasted some years ago, they were getting lots of financing from Russia and that financing were illicit, that would be known to the Kremlin.

SIMPSON: I think-- I mean, yes, I think that's true. I think we had more specific reporting than that from Chris, and I think it's credible.

SIMPSON: There was -- well, for one thing, there was various criminals were buying the properties. So there was a gangster -- a Russian gangster living in Trump Tower.

SCHIFF: Who was that?

SIMPSON: His gangster name is Taiwanchik. I couldn't spell his actual name. But, you know, I mean, these are the kind of things that prompted us to hire Mr. Steele.

We had a gangster named Taiwanchik living in Trump Tower who had been under-- I'm sorry, he was -- **I think he was running** a -- his associates were living in Trump Tower, and he was running a high-stakes gambling ring out of Trump Tower, while he himself was a fugitive for having rigged the skating competition at the Salt Lake Olympics and a bunch of other sporting events engaged in rigging.

And when Mr. Trump went to the Miss Universe pageant in 2013, Taiwanchik was there in the VIP section with Mr. Trump and lots of other Kremlin biggies. So that kind of thing raised questions with us...

SCHIFF: And **tell me about the Trump Hollywood project**... Did they get the financing from what you could tell because they got a bunch of Russians to presale, or did they go to a bank and say these are our investors, or how did they go about that?

SIMPSON: Well, eventually, I mean, they lost the project. **It went under.** I, can't - I'm not - I'm sure we did look at who the creditors were, who the lenders were.

SCHIFF: And when you talk about the **connection between the Trump campaign and the Brexit campaign,** is that a line you're drawing through Cambridge Analytica, or were there other lines you were drawing there?

SIMPSON: Well, **Bannon went over to the UK in or around 2011.** And originally, he was trying to set up a sort of British tea party, which was an inopportune choice of...

SCHIFF: And, I mean, were you able to find any factual links between the Mercers and Assange or Wikileaks or Farage?

SIMPSON: Well, I mean, the things that we heard, which, you know, I think could be sorted out by an official inquiry are that Nigel Farage made a number of trips to New York and had a number of meetings -

B. BRENNAN – CIA. CONSPIRACY

On 23 MAY 2017, Former CIA Director John O. Brennan testified before HPSCI. Here are some excerpts regarding Russian collusion:

REP. ADAM SCHIFF (D), CALIFORNIA:
Have any members of the IC shared with you their concerns that the president was attempting to enlist the help of people within the intelligence community to **drop the Flynn investigation?**

BRENNAN: No, sir.

SCHIFF: Are you aware of any efforts the president has made to enlist the support of intelligence community personnel to **push back on a narrative involving the collusion** issue that Mr. Rooney was asking about?

BRENNAN: I am unaware of it.

REP. TERRI SEWELL (D), ALABAMA:
Have you seen the Trump administration do anything to push back, as you said? Have you seen or witnessed -- I know that you're no longer in the -- you know, no longer a director, but have you seen any indication that we're trying to punish or stop the Russians from doing this again?

BRENNAN: I'm not a position to evaluate, because there could be things going on behind the scenes. We were doing things behind the scenes to -- to try to counter Russian activities.

REP. JACKIE SPEIER (D), CALIFORNIA:
I'd like to spend some time talking about the outsized role that the Russian oligarchy plays in terms of supporting the Russian government. It's been said that there -- when the Russians want to cultivate a U.S. person, they will do it over a long period of time. Is that your experience?

BRENNAN: I guess (ph) a lot depends on the U.S. person and their willingness to work with the Russians.

SPEIER: Were you aware that they were attempting to cultivate then-real estate developer Donald Trump for almost eight years?

BRENNAN: I'm not going to talk about any individuals.

For the Forgotten Americans

CIA - DIR. BRENNAN

"I don't have sufficient information to make a determination whether or not such cooperation or complicity or collusion was taking place."

Former CIA Director Brennan

"If someone saw what you saw, and only what you saw, with respect to those (Trump) contacts -- if they looked at the intelligence that you saw... and then they characterize what they saw as having been evidence of collusion or collaboration, they'd be misrepresenting the intelligence would they not? ...
Only what you saw. They would be misrepresenting the intelligence, correct?"

Congressman Turner (R-OH)

"I presume they would be misrepresenting what it is that I saw. "

Former CIA Director Brennan

SPEIER: So were any of the oligarchs investing in U.S. properties owned by then-real estate developer Trump?

BRENNAN: I don't know the answer to that question.

SPEIER: There have been reports in newspapers that British and Dutch intelligence had provided information about meetings in European cities between Russian officials associated with President Putin and associates of the Trump campaign. Is that how you first found out about those meetings?

BRENNAN: I am not going to talk about anything that any of our international partners might have shared with us.

SPEIER: All right.

REP. ERIC SWALWELL (D), CALIFORNIA:

With respect to the contacts between Russia and Trump campaign persons...and whether they were innocent or benign contacts, when you see a multiplicity of contacts between one country and one campaign, when does it -- in your mind, when you're deciding whether to refer it to the FBI -- when does it move from mere coincidences to a pattern? And in this case, when did it?

BRENNAN: I guess -- it's all sort of very sui generis, as far as the instances are concerned... We don't have a totality of insight into all the things the Russians were doing. And I left it up to the professionals -- the counterintelligence and Russian experts -- to make sure that whatever information that they deemed appropriate to share with the Bureau because it could be relevant to their investigation -- they did that.

REP. MIKE TURNER (R), OHIO:

If someone left this hearing today and said that you had indicated that those contacts were evidence of collusion or collaboration, they would be misrepresenting your statements, correct?

BRENNAN: They would have misheard my response to the very good questions that were asked of me.

TURNER: Would you say that's a misrepresentation of your statement, yes?

BRENNAN: I would say that it was not an accurate portrayal of my statement.

SWALWELL: May 10th of this year **produced an unsettling image inside the Oval Office.** President Trump, standing and laughing with Russia's

Ambassador Kislyak and Foreign Minister Lavrov. It's been further reported that President Trump shared highly sensitive codeword information with Russia, putting at risk U.S. lives and jeopardizing sources and methods. Are the Russians worthy of receiving such information in the manner alleged?

BRENNAN: I believe it's important for U.S. intelligence to provide to any of our foreign partners any information related to terrorist threats to foreign countries or their citizens. And that's why I authorized the provision of classified information numerous times to the Russians that I believe saved Russian lives...

REP. WENSTRUP (R) OHIO:

...I can't help but think back to the previous election, when we see on videotape, **President Obama says, "this is my last election. After my election, I have more flexibility**." And President Medvedev, who he's speaking to, says, "I understand. I'll transmit this information to Vladimir, and I stand with you."

This is certainly an influential American, and we're talking openly about elections.. So you weren't sitting as a director at that time, but, **you know, as Mr. Swalwell used the term, that's a pretty disturbing image.**

So would you question this interaction, where that type of conversation's taking place?

BRENNAN: I try to avoid getting involved in political issues, partisan issues.

REP. TOM ROONEY (R), FLORIDA:

Did you find direct evidence of collusion between the Trump campaign and Putin in Moscow while you were there?

BRENNAN: Mr. Rooney, I never was an FBI agent I never was a prosecutor so I really don't do evidence; I do intelligence throughout the course of my career. As an intelligence professional, what we try to do is to make sure that we provide all relevant information to the bureau if there is an investigation underway that they're looking into criminal activity.

ROONEY: With regard to hacking, when did you learn of the Russian hacking in the last election cycle?

BRENNAN: ... in the summer.

ROONEY: Are you aware that both campaigns were notified at that time that there was an effort by the Russians to hack and try to influence the -- the political campaign of -- of last year?

BRENNAN: I was aware that both campaigns were being contacted and notified about it, yes...

REP. TREY GOWDY (R), SOUTH CAROLINA:

Do you know who commissioned The Steele Dossier?

BRENNAN: I don't.

GOWDY: Do you know if the FBI paid for any -- portion of The Steele dossier?

BRENNAN: I don't know. I know there are press reports related to that, but I -- I don't know, I have no firsthand knowledge of that.

GOWDY: Do you know whether any of the underlying allegations made in The Steele Dossier were other ever tested, probed, examined, cross-examined, whether the sources were examined for reliability, credibility?

BRENNAN: I know that there were efforts made by the Bureau to try to understand whether or not any of the information in that was valid, but I just -- I don't have any firsthand knowledge of it.

GOWDY: Do you know if the Bureau ever relied on The Steele Dossier as part of any court filings, applications, petitions, pleadings?

BRENNAN: I have no awareness.

GOWDY: Did the CIA rely on it?

BRENNAN: No.

GOWDY: Why not?

BRENNAN: Because we -- we didn't, it wasn't part of the corpus of intelligence information that we had. It was not in any way used as a basis for the intelligence community assessment that was done. It was -- it was not. When you learned of Russian efforts, did you have evidence of a connection between the Trump campaign and Russian state actors?

BRENNAN: As I said Mr. Gowdy, I don't do evidence...

GOWDY: Well, I...

BRENNAN: ... and we were uncovering information intelligence about interactions and contacts between U.S. persons and the Russians. And as we came upon that, we would share it with the bureau.

GOWDY: I appreciate that you don't do evidence, Director Brennan. Unfortunately, that's what I do. That's the word we use, you use the word assessment, you use the word tradecraft. I use the word evidence. And the good news for me is lots of my colleagues on the other side of the aisle use the word evidence, too.

One of my colleagues said there is more than circumstantial evidence of collusion between the Russians and the Trump campaign. Now, there are only two types of evidence; there's circumstantial and direct. ... Those aren't my words; those are the words of one of my colleagues on the other side of this very committee. Another Democrat colleague also used the word evidence, that he has seen evidence of collusion between the Trump campaign and the Russians and yet a third California Democrat, said she had seen no evidence of collusion.

So that's three different members of Congress from the same state, using the same word, **which is evidence.** And that's the word that my fellow citizens understand, evidence.

Assessment is -- is your vernacular. Tradecraft is your vernacular.

You and I both know the worth the word evidence makes.

We're not getting into whether or not you corroborated, contradicted, examined, cross-examined. We're not getting into how you tested and probed the reliability of that evidence; it's a really simple question.

Did evidence exist of collusion, coordination, conspiracy, between the Trump campaign and Russian state actors at the time you learned of 2016 efforts?

BRENNAN: I encountered and am aware of information and intelligence that revealed contacts and interactions between Russian officials and U.S. persons involved in the Trump campaign that I was concerned about because of known Russian efforts to suborn such individuals and it raised questions in my mind, again, whether or not the Russians were able to gain the cooperation of those individuals.

I don't know whether or not such collusion -- and that's your term, such collusion existed. I don't know.

But I know that there was a sufficient basis of information and intelligence that required further investigation by the bureau to determine whether or not U.S. persons were actively conspiring, colluding with Russian officials.

GOWDY: How did you test, probe, examine, cross-examine, otherwise test the reliability or believability, credibility, of that evidence you uncovered?

BRENNAN: I made sure that the components within CIA that have responsible for counterintelligence, cyber, and Russia, were actively working to understand as much as possible about the reliability, accuracy of the information that they already collected and information that was available needed further corroboration.

GOWDY: All right, well, there are a bunch of words that start with C floating around. I asked you about collusion, coordination and conspiracy, and you used the word "contact." ...So was it contact that you saw? Was it something more than contact? What is the nature of what you saw?

BRENNAN: I saw interaction and -- aware of interaction that, again, raised questions in my mind about what was the true nature of it. **But I don't know. I don't have sufficient information to make a determination whether or not such cooperation or complicity or collusion was taking place.** But I know that there was a basis to have individuals pull those threads.

GOWDY: ...but you saw something that led you to refer it to law enforcement, and in your judgment, it is up to law enforcement to test, probe, corroborate, contradict, otherwise investigate the full nature of that information you passed on. Is that a fair way to put it?

BRENNAN: Yes, it is because it's not CIA's job to make a determination about whether a U.S. person is cooperating, colluding, or whatever in some type of criminal or legal matter. It is our responsibility to give the Bureau everything that they need in order to follow that path and make such a determination and recommendation if they want to press charges.

GOWDY: Did you also refer to Director Clapper?

BRENNAN: Not everything that was shared with the Bureau was shared with Director Clapper.

GOWDY: And why would that be?

BRENNAN: Because, on counterintelligence matters dealing with U.S. person information of a very sensitive nature, the Office of the DNI and the DNI does not have that type of operational responsibility. And what we try to do is to make sure that there is as little exposure of that information as possible. I would keep General Clapper informed about the nature of my engagements,.

GOWDY: With as much specificity as you can give us, when did you refer that information to the Bureau?

BRENNAN: Would you accept last year as the answer? It was during the summertime, and the...

GOWDY: OK.

BRENNAN:...but even previously, there are ongoing sharing of information with the -- the Bureau, and so it was over the course of the -- of the year.

GOWDY: in the summer, you shared the information with Director Comey at the Bureau?

BRENNAN: Sometime this summer, there was information that the CIA had that was shared with the Bureau. But it wasn't the only period of time where such information was shared with the Bureau.

BRENNAN: That's correct.

GOWDY: Have you ever requested that a U.S. person's name be unmasked?

BRENNAN: Yes I have.

GOWDY: Have you also either approved or denied requests of others that a U.S. person's name be unmasked?

BRENNAN: I don't recall in my tenure at CIA any decision on unmasking for someone else coming up to my level...

GOWDY: Do you recall any U.S. ambassadors asking that names be unmasked?

BRENNAN: I don't -- I don't know. Maybe it's ringing a vague bell but I'm not -- I could not answer with any confidence.

GOWDY: Do you remember what your last day on the job was at the CIA? What was the date?

BRENNAN: It was noon on January 20 when I gave up my responsibility as director of CIA.

GOWDY: On either January 19 or up till noon on January 20, did you make any unmasking requests?

BRENNAN: I do not believe I did.

GOWDY: So you did not make any requests on the last day that you were employed?

BRENNAN: No, I was not in the agency on the last day I was employed. I definitely know that on the last day I was employed I definitely did not make such a request.

C. COMEY – FBI. OBSTRUCTION?

James Brien Comey, Jr. – the 7th Director of the Federal Bureau of Investigation – was under oath before Congress: at the HPSCI 20 MARCH 2017, at the Senate Judiciary Committee 03 MAY 2017, and the Senate Intelligence Committee on 08 JUNE 2017.

With answers like "I cannot comment on that" and "I cannot comment on an ongoing investigation", Comey's first two testimonies provided little information to the public. However, after being fired in May, the former FBI Director had much more to say on 08 JUNE. Here are some excerpts regarding the investigation into Russian collusion with Trump and his campaign:

CHAIRMAN RICHARD BURR – NORTH CAROLINA (R):

Do you have any doubt that Russia attempted to interfere In the 2016 election?

COMEY: None.

BURR: Do you have any doubt that the Russian government was behind the cyber intrusion in the state voter files?

COMEY: No.

BURR: Are you confident that no votes cast in the 2016 presidential election were altered?

COMEY: I'm confident. When I left as director I had seen no indication of that whatever.

BURR: Did the president at any time ask you to stop the FBI Investigation into Russian involvement in the 2016 U.S. elections?

COMEY: Not to my understanding, no.

Burr: Did any individual working for this administration, including the Justice Department, ask you to stop the Russian investigation?

COMEY: No.

SENATOR DIANE FEINSTEIN – (D- CA):

FEINSTEIN: Why do you believe you were fired?

COMEY: I guess I don't know for sure. I believe — I think the President at his word, I was fired because of the Russian investigation, something about the way I was conducting it, the President felt created pressure on him that he wanted to relieve. Again, I didn't know that at the time, but I watched his interview, read the press accounts of his conversations, so I take him at his word there.

Look, I could be wrong. Maybe he's saying something that is not true, but I take him at his word, at least based on what I know now.

FEINSTEIN: Do you believe the Russia investigation played a role?

COMEY: In why I was fired?

FEINSTEIN: Yes.

COMEY: Yes, because I've seen the President say so.

FEINSTEIN: You described two phone calls that you received from President Trump. One on March 30, and one on April 11th, where he, quote, **described the Russia investigation** as a cloud that was impairing his ability, end quote, as President and asked you, quote, to **lift the cloud**, end quote. What — how did you interpret that and what did you believe he wanted you to do.

COMEY: I interpreted that as he was frustrated that the Russia investigation was taking up so much time and energy. I think he meant of the executive branch, but in the public square in general and making it difficult to focus on other priorities of his. What he asked me was actually narrower than that. I think what he meant by the cloud, I could be wrong, but what I think he meant by the cloud was the entire investigation is taking up oxygen and making it hard for me to focus on the things I want to focus on. The ask was, to get it out that I, the President, am not personally under investigation.

FEINSTEIN: After April 11th, did he ask you more ever about the Russia investigation? Did he ask you any questions?

COMEY: We never spoke again after April 11th. That was a slightly cowardly way to avoid telling him we're not going to do that....

SENATOR MARCO RUBIO – (R- FL):

On the cloud, we keep talking about this cloud, you perceive the cloud to be the Russian investigation in general.

COMEY: Yes, sir.

RUBIO: But his specific ask was that you would tell the American people what you had already told him, what you had already told the leaders of congress, both Democrats and Republicans, that he was not personally under investigation.

COMEY: Yes, sir.

RUBIO: He was asking you to do what you have done here today?

COMEY: Correct, yes, sir.

RUBIO: Okay. And, again, at that setting, did you say to the President, that it would be inappropriate for you to do so and talk to the White House counsel or anybody so they would hopefully talk to him and tell him he couldn't do this?

COMEY: First time I said I'll see what we can do, second time, I explained how it should work that the white house counsel should contact the deputy attorney general.

RUBIO: You told him —

COMEY: The President said, okay, I think that's what I'll do.

RUBIO: On a number of occasions here, you bring up — let's talk about the general Russia investigation, okay. And page six of your testimony **you say, the first thing you say is he asked what we could do to quote/unquote lift the cloud, the general Russia investigation** and you responded that we were investigating the matter as quickly as we could and that there would be great benefit if we didn't find anything to having done the work well and he agreed. He re-emphasized the problems it was causing him but agreed. The President agreed with your statement it would be great if we could have an investigation all the facts came out, and we found nothing. So he agreed that would be ideal, but this cloud is still messing up my ability to do the rest of my agenda, Is that an accurate assessment?

COMEY: Yes, he went further than that. He said if some of my satellites did something wrong, It would be good to find that out.

RUBIO: That's the second part. That is the satellites. He said if one of my satellites, I imagine by that he meant some of the other people surrounding his campaign did something wrong, It would be great to know that as well.

COMEY: Yes, sir, that's what he said.

For the Forgotten Americans

RUBIO: Are those the other — only two instances in which that sort of back and forth happened where the President was basically saying, I'm paraphrasing here, **It is okay, do the Russia investigation, I hope it all comes out, I have nothing to do with anything Russia, and it would be great if all came out, If people around me were doing things that were wrong.**

Comey: Yes, as I recorded it accurately, that was the sentiment he was expressing.

SENATOR JAMES RISCH – (R- ID):

… I gather from all this that you're willing to say now that while you were director the president of the United States was not under investigation, Is that a fair statement?

COMEY: That's correct.

Risch: That's a fact we can rely on?

COMEY: Yes, sir.

RISCH: I remember you talked with us shortly after February 14th when "The New York Times" wrote an article that suggested that the Trump campaign was colluding with the Russians. You remember reading that article when it came out?

COMEY: I do it was about extensive electronic surveillance.

RISCH: Correct. That upset you to the point where you went out and surveyed the intelligence community to see whether you were missing something in that, Is that correct?

COMEY: That's correct. I want to be careful in open setting —

RISCH: I'm not going to go any further than that, so thank you. In addition to that, after that, you sought out, both Republican and Democrat Senators to tell them that, hey, I don't know where this is coming from, but this is not the case.

This is not factual. Do you recall that?

COMEY: Yes.

RISCH: Okay. So the American people can understand this, that report by "the new york times" was not true, Is that fair statement?

COMEY: **It was not true.** Again, all of you know this, maybe the American people don't. The challenge — I'm not picking on reporters about writing stories about classified information. That people talking about it often don't really know what's going on and those of us who actually know what's going on are not talking about it and we don't call the press to say, hey, you got that thing wrong about this sensitive topic, we just have to leave it there, mention the chairman and the nonsense about what influenced me to make the July 5th statement, nonsense. But I can't go explaining how it is nonsense.

<u>VICE CHAIRMAN MARK WARNER – VIRGINIA (D):</u>

Did he ever ask about you trying to interfere on any other investigation?

COMEY: No.

COMEY: I'm sitting here going through my contacts. I had one conversation with the president that was classified where he asked about our — an ongoing intelligence investigation, it was brief and entirely professional.

WARNER: He didn't ask you to take any specific action?

COMEY: No.

WARNER: Unlike what he had done vis-à-vis Admiral Flynn?

COMEY: No.

GENERAL FLYNN

WARNER: The president seems from, my reading of your memo, to be holding your job or your possibility of continuing your job over your head in a fairly direct way. What was your impression and what did you mean by this notion of a patronage relationship?

COMEY: ...again, it's my impression, I could always be wrong. My commonsense told me that what was going on is either he had concluded or someone had told him that you didn't — you've already asked Comey to stay and you didn't get anything for it.

RISCH: On page five, paragraph three, you put this in quotes, words matter, you wrote down the words so we can have the words in front of us now. 28 words in quotes, It says, quote, I hope, this is the president speaking, I hope you can see your way clear to letting this go, to letting Flynn go. He's a good guy. I hope you can let this go. Now, those are his exact words, is that correct?

COMEY: Correct.

RISCH: You wrote them here and put them in quotes.

COMEY: Correct.

RISCH: Thank you for that. He did not direct you to let it go.

COMEY: Not in his words, no.

RISCH: He did not order you to let it go.

COMEY: Again, those words are not an order.

RISCH: He said I hope...Do you know of any case where a person has been charged for obstruction of justice or for that matter any other criminal offense where this — they said or thought they hoped for an outcome?

COMEY: I don't know well enough to answer. And the reason I keep saying his words is I took it as a direction. It is the President of the United States, with me alone, saying I hope this, I took it as this is what he wants me to do. I didn't obey that, but that's the way I took it.

RISCH: You may have taken it as a direction, but **that's not what he said. He said — he said I hope.**

COMEY: Those are the exact words, correct.

RISCH: You don't know of anyone that has ever been charging for hoping something, is that a fair statement.

COMEY: I don't as I sit here.

FEINSTEIN: Let's go to the Flynn issue. Senator Risch outlined, I hope you can see your way to letting Flynn go, he's a good guy, I hope you can let this go. But you also said in your written remarks and I quote, that you had understood the President to be requesting that we drop any investigation of Flynn in connection with false statements about his conversations with the Russian ambassador in December, end quote. Please go into that with more detail.

COMEY: Well, the context and the President's words are what led me to that conclusion, as I said in my statement, I could be wrong, but Flynn had been forced to resign the day before. And the controversy around general Flynn at that point in time was centered on whether he had lied to the vice President about the nature of his conversations with the Russians, whether he had been candid with others in the course of that, and so that happens on the day before on the 14th the President makes specific reference to that, and so that's why I understood him to be saying what he wanted me to do was drop any investigation connected to Flynn's account of his conversations with the Russians.

FEINSTEIN: Now, here's the question. You're big, you're strong... But why didn't you stop and say, Mr. President, this is wrong? I cannot discuss this with you.

COMEY: It is a great question. Maybe if I were stronger I would have, I was so stunned by the conversation that I just took it In...Maybe other people would be stronger in that circumstance. But that was — that's how I conducted myself. I hope I never have another opportunity, maybe if I did it again, I would do it better.

RUBIO: Thank you. Director Comey, the meeting in the oval office where he made the request about mike Flynn, was that the only time he asked you to hopefully let it go?

COMEY: Yes.

RUBIO: And in that meeting as you understood it, that was — he was asking not about the general Russia investigation, he was asking very specifically about the jeopardy that Flynn was in himself.

COMEY: That's how I understood it, yes, sir.

RUBIO: As you perceived it, while he was a request that you hoped you would do away with it, you perceived it as an order?

COMEY: Yes.

RUBIO: At the time did you say anything to the President about that, that's not an appropriate request or tell the White House counsel that is not an appropriate request, someone needs to tell the President that he can't do these things?

COMEY: I didn't, no.

RUBIO: Okay. Why?

COMEY: I don't know. I think the — as I said earlier, I think the circumstances were such, I was a bit stunned and didn't have the presence of mind and I don't know, I don't want to make you sound like I'm captain courageous, I don't know whether if I had the presence of mind, I would have said, sir, that's wrong. I don't know whether I would have. In the moment, It didn't come to my mind, what came to my mind is be careful what you say and so I said, I agree Flynn is a good guy.

RUBIO: On March 30th, during the phone call about general Flynn, you said he abruptly shifted and brought up something that you call quote/unquote **the McCabe thing**, specifically the McCabe thing as you understood it was that McCabe's wife received campaign money from what I assume mean Terry McAuliffe?

COMEY: Yes, sir.

RUBIO: And so why did you — had the President at any point in time expressed to you concern, opposition, potential opposition to McCabe, I don't like this guy, he got money from someone close to Clinton.

COMEY: He asked me during previous conversations about Andy Mccabe. And said in essence how is he going to be with me as President. I was rough on him on the campaign trail.

RUBIO: Rough on McCabe?

COMEY: By his own account, he said he was rough on McCabe and Mr. McCabe on the campaign trail, how is he going to be? I assured the President Andy is a total pro, no issue at all, you got to note people at the FBI, they are not —

RUBIO: Finally, who are those senior leaders at the FBI that you share these conversations with?

COMEY: As I said in response to Senator Feinstein's question, deputy director, my chief of staff, general counsel, deputy directors, chief counsel, and then more often than not the number three person at the FBI, the associate deputy director, and then quite often head of the national security branch.

LETS LOOK AT COMEY'S SENIOR LEADERS

James Comey	Director	Fired
Andrew McCabe	Deputy Director	Fired
James Rybicki	Chief of Staff	Departed
James Baker	FBI General Counsel	Resigned
Michael Kortan	Assistant Director	Retired
Peter Strzok	Assoc. Deputy Director	Fired
Other Key Figures:		
Lisa Page	FBI/DOJ Attorney	Resigned
	Part of Mueller's team	
Bruce Ohr	once DOJ's "No.4"	Demoted
Josh Campbell	Special Asst. to Comey	Resigned

CHAPTER 14

ALL ABOUT FUSION GPS

SIMPSON SAYS

We (Fusion GPS) generally are all ex-journalists

I don't specifically remember, but what I can say is that the Clinton Foundation and related issues has come up in my work a lot.

No one hired me to investigate Hillary Clinton in 2015 or 2016.

WHO IS GLENN SIMPSON?

[Patrick Davis, Deputy Chief Investigative Counsel for Chairman Grassley:

Q: Mr. Simpson, what is your professional background?

A: I have a degree in journalism from George Washington University and I've spent most of my working adult life as a journalist, much of it as an investigative reporter for the Wall Street Journal. Prior to that I worked as an investigative reporter at Roll Call Newspaper…

Q: And when did you leave the Wall Street Journal?

A: In 2009.

WHO IS FUSION GPS AND WHAT DO THEY DO?

Q: What is Bean, LLC?

A: That's the LLC that is my current company.

Q: And what is your role in Bean, LLC?

A: I'm the majority owner.   I guess, you know, we don't have official titles, but I'm generally referred to as the CEO.

Q: Bean, LLC registered Fusion GPS as a trade name in the District of Columbia; is that correct?

A: Yes, it's a DBA.

Q: Why did you choose to use a trade name for Bean, LLC rather than directly name the company Fusion GPS?

A: Because at the time that I was deciding what I wanted to do I was recruiting a new partner and I just needed to set up a holding company while I organized my new business. So I just picked a name….

Q: Is Bean, LLC currently registered in D.C. to conduct business under the trade name Fusion GPS?

A: To my knowledge it is. It should be.

Q: Have any other LLC's or business entities conducted business as Fusion GPS?

A: I don't think so.

Q: Have any other LLC's or business entities received payments for work conducted by Fusion GPS, its employees, or its associates?

MR. LEVY [Joshua Levy, Cunningham Levy Muse and Counsel of Simpson]: Are you asking to include subcontractors or are you --

MR. DAVIS: Sure.

MR. LEVY: Does Fusion GPS have subcontractors?

MR. DAVIS: Right. I think that would be part of it, but the other part is: are there other LLC's associated with Bean direct- -- with Bean or Fusion directly, not just subcontractors?

BY THE WITNESS [SIMPSON]:

A: Yes. I mean, the one I think that has come up in some of the correspondence or somewhere, I can't remember where, is another one called Kernel, K-E-R-N-E-L, and that was an LLC that was set up for a book project that never -- we never finished -- we never did the book. So it's inactive with the current time. Then there's another one that one of my partners manages that's for different types of work, technology, policy, and that type of thing.

Q: What's the name of that one?

A: I think it's Caudex, C-A-U-D-E-X.

Q: And are any other LLC's or types of business entities otherwise associated with Fusion GPS?

A: Those are the only ones I can think of.

Q: And have you been a registered agent, owner, or beneficial owner of any other LLC's or business entities?

A: I own an LLC in Maryland that holds some property that I own.

Q: And what's the name of that LLC?

A: As we sit here, I wasn't prepared for this question. I don't remember the name of it. It was registered fairly recently. Obviously we can get that to you.

Q: So is it correct that Fusion has at times worked with different LLC's based on by project?

A: For most of the history of the company Bean, LLC was the primary entity through which we did business. I'm not sure I totally understand your question. There's this other LLC I mentioned that's fairly recent and there may be other entities, but nothing that I, myself set up, at least not that I can think of.

Q: Where is Fusion GPS's physical office, if any?

A: DuPont Circle.

Q: Is it, if I recall correctly, 1700 Connecticut Avenue, Northwest?

A: That's the address, yes.

Q: Is it Suite 400?

A: It is.

Q: How many employees, associates does Fusion GPS currently have?

A: Roughly a dozen. [NAMES REDACTED]

Q: In general, what is Fusion GPS's business?

For the Forgotten Americans

A: We primarily are a research, strategy, consulting firm.

Q: And what types of clients has Fusion GPS had?

A: It runs the gamut from corporations to law firms, various investment funds, people involved in litigation. And roughly how many active clients did Fusion GPS have in 2016? That's difficult for me to answer. You know, over ten I would say, but it's hard for me -- beyond that I would be guessing.

Q: Does part of Fusion GPS's business involve attempting to have media outlets publish articles that further the interests of your clients?

A: Yeah, you could -- I mean, generally speaking, we are -- generally we tend to respond to inquiries more than try to push things, but, you know, we work with the press frequently.

Q: Has Fusion ever provided information to journalists in order to encourage them to publish articles or air stories that further your client's interests?

A: Yes.

Q: And has Fusion GPS provided information to journalists or editors in order to discourage them from publishing or airing stories that are contrary to your client's interests?

A: Well, what we -- we're a research company. So generally what we do is provide people with factual information. Our specialty is public record information. So if we get an inquiry about a story and some of the information that a reporter's presuming is incorrect and we give them correct information that may cause them to not write the story.

Q: Has Fusion GPS ever had arrangements with clients in which the amount of compensation was dependent on getting articles published or stories aired?

A: Not that I can recall.

Q: Has Fusion GPS ever had arrangements with clients in which the amount of Fusion's compensation was dependent upon preventing articles from being published or stories from being aired?

A: No, I don't think so, not to my recollection.

Q: To the best of your knowledge, has anyone associated with Fusion GPS ever told clients or prospective clients that the company could find and distribute information or take other actions in order to encourage government agencies to initiate an investigation?

A: Could you restate that?

Q: To the best of your knowledge, has anyone associated with Fusion GPS ever told clients or prospective clients that the company could find and distribute information or take other actions in order to encourage government agencies to initiate an investigation?

MR. LEVY: Within the scope of this interview?

MR. DAVIS: In general. I'm not asking about any particular case.

MR. LEVY: Hold on. Let's -- let me just talk to my client about that and get back to you on that. I just want to understand the facts so we can evaluate whether it's appropriate to discuss that here if such a predicate for the answer exists.

MR. FOSTER: [Jason Foster, Chief Investigative Counsel, Chairman Grassley]: Do you want to take a break?

MR. LEVY: Sure.

MR. FOSTER: Let's go off the record. It's 9:55.

(A short break was had.)

MR. DAVIS: We'll go back on the record. It's 10:02.

Q: After conferring with counsel, are you able to answer the question?

A: Yes. Could you just state it one more time.

Q: Sure. To the best of your knowledge, has anyone associated with Fusion GPS ever told clients or prospective clients that the company could find and distribute information or take other actions in order to encourage government agencies to initiate an investigation?

A: The word "associated" is really vague. I'm not sure I know what you mean by that.

I can speak to my own practices and the practices of the people who work at my company.

Generally speaking, when we do a research project for a new client and they ask us – you know, they explain, you know, what situation they're involved in, if it's a lawsuit, for example, or some other dispute, a lot of what we do is related to disputes, they say -- you know, we say we will conduct an open-ended inquiry that's not goal directed and the results of the research will guide whatever decision you want to make about how to use it.

So the range of possibilities with, you know, research are you could file a lawsuit, you could put it in a court filing, you could take it to a government agency, you could give it to Congress, you could give it to the press, but you don't really prejudge, you know, how you're going to use information until you know what you've got.

So we generally don't let our clients dictate sort of the -- you know, the end result of things because we don't think that's an intelligent way of trying to do research and, you know, a lot of what we do is decision support.

Your clients are frequently trying to make a decision about how they want to proceed, whether they want to -- you know, if someone thinks they've been defrauded, you can file a lawsuit, you can go to the police.

You would decide that based on what you find out about the, you know, evidence of a fraud. So that's generally the way we do it.

Q: To the best of your knowledge, has Fusion GPS ever had an arrangement with a client in which the company was specifically tasked with getting government agencies to initiate an investigation?

A: I would -- to the best of my recollection, we don't have any agreements like that we would put into writing generally for the reasons I stated in answer to the previous question. In the course of, you know, dealing with a client we might talk about whether, you know, something was worthy of a government investigation and talk about how that could be done. There's any number of scenarios there that might come under discussion, but, as I say, that's generally not how we frame a project.

Q: Has Fusion GPS ever had arrangements with clients in which the amount of Fusion's compensation was dependent on government agencies initiating an investigation?

A: We've been in business since 2010, so seven years is a fairly long time, but as I say, not to my recollection. I just can't be categorical because we've done a lot of work over the last seven years.

BY MS. SAWYER [Chief Oversight Counsel, Senator Feinstein]

Mr. Simpson, again, I'm Heather Sawyer, I work as counsel for Senator Feinstein, and I have with me two of my colleagues. I will primarily be asking the questions. They may have some follow-up...

Q: You had talked with my colleagues a bit about the work that Fusion GPS does in general and I wanted to ask you some follow-up on that. What would you describe as kind of the key expertise of your firm, Fusion GPS?

A: Public information is our specialty. We generally are all ex-journalists and specific type of journalists, investigative reporters, and, you know, being a journalist is all about finding public information. At least, you know, the kind of journalism I practiced was based on documents. I'm a document hound and so are my colleagues.

So essentially we gather up large quantities of public information and we process that. We've sort of more recently branched into data science and, you know, digital data, obtaining databases through FOIA. We do a lot of Freedom of Information Act (FOIA). We work with court records a lot, corporate records a lot. Some of my employees do a lot of financial crime and money laundering and fraud investigations, tax evasion, that sort of thing. Those are my specialties.

I was also a political reporter and covered campaigns and elections. I know a lot about how campaigns work and how, you know, Washington works generally. So we do things like policy disputes, one industry versus another, one company versus another.

We don't do a lot of campaign consulting, but **every four years for the last couple of cycles** we've done some presidential work. Generally speaking, the way our business is structured most campaigns don't have the budget for the kind of services that we provide. So we only would do things where people have the resources to pay for a serious piece of research. So we do things like a California initiative or presidential.

Q: And how would you describe like how would you pitch and why would a client need your services?

A: Generally speaking, people tend to get referred to us when they have a sort of undefined need, like they feel like they don't know what happened or they don't know what happened, they don't know what's going on.

So I think that's what I referred to earlier as the decision support part of our work. You know, a client will come to us and they'll say I'm being sued and they're accusing me of X and, you know, not only did I not do it, but I don't even understand why they're suing me. I mean, that's a kind of typical thing.

Also another example would be I think I've been defrauded, but I can't figure out how or why. Or I keep — you know, I run the best company in my industry and, you know, we make the best widgets and we keep losing out on the Pentagon contract to this other guy and we think something fishy's going on and we want you to help us figure it out.

Q: So in some ways it's fact gathering and due diligence for clients?

A: **Well, it is certainly fact gathering and I certainly am around the due diligence industry and I am essentially part of it, but we don't really do a lot of classic due diligence,** which has become a commoditized product in the business intelligence field that is conducted, you know, at a fairly sort of low level. It's become sort of a mass product like a McDonald's cheeseburger.

Q: I think when you were speaking with my colleagues you described your work as open ended and not results directed. Can you explain a little more what you mean by that?

A: Sure. Another thing we say about our work is it's custom information, it's a customized product.

You tell us what your problem is and we customize a research solution. In general when people come to us and they tell us what their challenge is, we stipulate that they retain us for 30 days, they agree to pay our fee, they don't tell us what to do, they don't tell us, you know, what result to get. I like to call it a holistic methodology.

The reason we do it that way, you know, **(A).** We are professionals and we feel like it's not helpful to have someone dictating how you do things, but, **(B).** If you predetermine the result that you're looking for you tend to miss things.

So it's better -- you know, it's pure versus applied science, right? You're looking to understand how things work before you understand what you might need to address a particular problem. What happens after you've done open-ended research is then, of course, you try to apply it to the specific issues at hand. So if you're not able to get a government contract and you think the other guy is up to something and we find out, you know, indeed he's been making, you know, payments to somebody, you know, then we would, you know, advise them on how to address that.

Q: So the way it's structured you are certainly free to follow the facts wherever they may lead you in the course of research?

A: That's right. You know, it's a little different in litigation where you're working for an attorney and he's got specific things he needs, like serving a witness or something like that, but on the research side of it it's -- I have the professional -- basically I reserve for myself the professional freedom to find out the answers.

Q: A January 11, 2017, "New York Times" article described your firm, Fusion GPS, as a firm that "Most often works for business clients, but in presidential elections the firm is sometimes hired by candidates, party organizations, or donors to do political "**oppo work**", opposition research on the side." Is that an accurate description of the firm?

A: In a shorthand way, yeah. I mean, it's consistent with the description I think I gave you. We don't do a lot of campaign work, but, you know, every few years we do. And most of our clients are not trying to win an election. They're trying to win a lawsuit or, you know, find out who ripped them off.

Q: With regard to the political or campaign work that you do, the same principles you've talked about in terms of how the relationship is structured, how the research is done, do those same principles apply to that political or campaign research as well?

A: Yes. There's a limited number of examples because we don't do a lot of it (campaign work), but, again, my specialty is really sort of financial investigations and business practices.

In the last -- you know, in a current example we have a businessman who had a far-flung business empire all around the world. So, you know, that was a natural subject for me. So we do, we investigate multinational enterprises on a frequent basis.

Q: Just to be clear, when you say "in the current example," what are you referring to?

A: 2016 presidential election.

Q: By extension, when you're talking about an international businessman, I presume you're talking about then candidate now President Trump?

A: Yes.

Q: I do want to ask you more about that, but before we get to that, in general, when you do the political or campaign work you're equally free to follow the facts wherever they lead you and the firm Fusion GPS?

A: Yes, that's right.

Q: Now, certainly it sounds like you handle business for multiple clients, not just one client at one time. How do you handle the fact that you have work for more than one client in terms of protecting confidentiality in general and ensuring -- well, first of all, I presume that you take steps so that work for one client is not shared with another client?

MR. LEVY: What's the question?

MS. SAWYER: Do you take steps to ensure that work that you're doing for one client is not shared with another client?

BY THE WITNESS [SIMPSON]:

A: Yes. My partners and I don't talk about -- it's like a lawyer wouldn't talk about one client to another client. You know, there's some exceptions when things become public. If we're working on a public matter and someone else asks us about it, I mean, obviously if it's public it's not -- it doesn't need to be protected.But we have systems to segregate our cases and clients and, you know, we deal with them individually and we operate in that sense, you know, like a lawyer would.

As the business has grown, you know, we've taken on more and more matters. So I don't – you know, I generally do about a half a dozen cases at a time on all range of subjects in all parts of the world, and the same is true of my partners and we divide them up. So sometimes we work together, but frequently each of them will be doing three, four, five cases at a time.

Q: With regard to subcontractors...do you have a policy that is shared with them about how they are to treat the information that they're doing on behalf of one of your clients vis-a-vis some of your other clients?

A: **Well, our subcontractors are governed by NDA's (Non-Disclosure Agreements) to start with.** In most cases that I can think of we don't have one subcontractor working on more than one matter, but to the extent that would happen, we don't really -- when you're dealing with subcontractors you're giving them generally very specific assignments, find out what you can about this company or this businessman or this court case, whatever, and a lot of that you never get into who the client is. It's irrelevant.

I'd say more often than not the subcontractors don't know who the client is.

For the Forgotten Americans

CHAPTER 15
FUSION GPS & TRUMP

SIMPSON SAYS

when we reached an agreement about, you know, funding and we thought we would have funding to do a bunch of things, we began to look for people who could help us pursue some of these things.

I don't know what to tell you other than that I was generally aware that Perkins Coie represented the DNC.

I knew it was the DNC that we were working for.

So from the very beginning of this organized crime was -- Russian organized crime was a focus of interest.

So, you know, I was sort of an amateur student of the subject (Russian mafia)...You know, Russian organized crime is very different from Italian organized crime.

We saw indications that some of the (Trump) money came from Kazakhstan, among other places, and that some of it you just couldn't account for.

FUSION GPS HIRED FOR RESEARCH ON TRUMP

MS. SAWYER continues:

Q: So you had mentioned a few minutes ago that you had done some political or campaign research in the course of the 2016 presidential election and you clarified that that was work related to then Candidate and now President Trump. <u>What can you tell us about that work? Can you just describe it first generally and then I'll ask you some follow-up</u>.

A: It was, broadly speaking, a kind of holistic examination of Donald Trump's business record and his associations, his bankruptcies, his suppliers, you know, offshore or third-world suppliers of products that he was selling. You know, it evolved somewhat quickly into issues of his relationships to organized crime figures but, you know, really the gamut of Donald Trump.

What we generally do at the beginning of a case if it's possible is to order all the books about the subject from Amazon so we're not reinventing the wheel and we know what's been written and said before. So this was typical. We ordered every Donald Trump book and, to my surprise, that's a lot of books.

I was never very interested in Donald Trump. He was not a serious political figure that I'd ever had any exposure to. He's a New York figure really.

So anyway, we read everything we could read about Donald Trump. Those books cover his divorces, his casinos, his early years dealings with labor unions and mafia figures. I'm trying to think what else.

His (Trump's) exes (former wives) certainly have always been a big issue. Again, it was sort of an unlimited look at his -- you know, his business and finances and that sort of thing.

Q: <u>And when did this work begin</u>?

A: **It was either September or October of 2015**.

I recall being in London on other business and hearing somebody wanted for us to take a look at it.

Q: <u>And what can you tell us about who engaged you initially to do that work</u>?

MR. LEVY: **The answer to that question might implicate privilege.**

BY MS. SAWYER:

Q: So it has been publicly reported that the initial engagement of September to October 2015 was by someone with ties -- with Republican ties. Can you confirm whether that is accurate or not?

MR. LEVY: **We're not going to talk about the identity of clients.**

BY MS. SAWYER:

Q: So with regard to this engagement in September -- that began initially in September or October 2015, what were you asked specifically to do?

For the Forgotten Americans

A: I don't have specific recollection of there being a specific tasking. I believe it was why don't you take a look at Donald Trump, it looks like he may, you know, be more successful than people think, something -- there was some level of insight that he had a better shot (winning the Republican nominee) than people were giving him at the time, but it was on open-ended request like most of the things that we get.

Q: And, again, on that one was the work directed at all by the client? Did they ask you to look at any particular aspects of Candidate Trump's background?

A: I don't -- I know there was –

MR. LEVY: We're not going to get into client communications. It's privileged.

BY MS. SAWYER:

Q: Were you in any way limited in the research that you did or the facts that you wanted to pursue?

A: Can I talk generally about my practices and the history?

Q: Sure.

A: I mean, in general it's very rare for someone to tell me look here, don't look there. For the most part we are looking at -- you know, we're trying to understand something big. So it's really counterproductive for somebody to tell you look here, don't look there, I'm interested in X but not Y.

So we generally sort of push back when that happens, but I have to say we sort of set the rules at the beginning and people, you know, accepted those terms. So generally that's what we explain to people in the beginning of our engagements, you know, let us do our jobs and that's the way it works best.

Q: And did that -- can you tell us whether that general practice and rule applied to the engagement that you took on in September or October 2015 with regard to Candidate Trump?

MR. LEVY: You can answer that without getting into client communications.

BY THE WITNESS [SIMPSON]:

A: I mean, we were -- it was regular order. As, you know, various people will tell you, I'm -- you know, it would be like herding a cat, right? We're going to do what we do. So it was regular order.

Q: And then when you spoke with my colleagues earlier you had indicated that sometimes when facts are gathered you present options to a client and you articulated kind of four options, a potential lawsuit, take it to a government agency, give it to Congress, give it to the press. Did you – were those the general options on the table with regard to this engagement as well?

MR. LEVY: If you can discuss it without talking about client communications. If you can't, you can't.

BY THE WITNESS [SIMPSON]:

A: I'm just trying to -- because it evolved it's a little bit hard to -- I mean, in the beginning of this case like pretty much every case there was no -- there was no range of options -- there weren't -- it was a request to see what we could find out about Donald Trump and the, you know, goal or sort of reason, there wasn't really one.

It was tell me what we need to know about this guy (Trump).

So later on, you know, we started getting press inquiries and at that point, you know, the sort of press element enters the equation, **but I can't really get into what they told me or didn't tell me to do.**

==

"THE WASHINGTON FREE BEACON"

CRITICAL INSERT: During the Senate exam, Simpson refused to reveal that the first client was "The Washington Free Beacon. The House Permanent Select Committee on Intelligence (HPSCI) identified it

[**NOTE:** Wikipedia states: *"The Washington Free Beacon" is an American conservative political journalism web site launched in 2012.*]

MR. GOWDY: Were you hired by a person or entity in either 2015 or 2016 to do research into then-candidate Donald Trump?

MR. SIMPSON: Yes, we were. We were hired around October, September-October of 2015.

MR. GOWDY: By whom?

MR. SIMPSON: The Free Beacon has been publicly stated as the client or identified to the committee as the client, and I can confirm that.

MR. GOWDY: All right. I'm going to be asking you questions even though there's been public reporting. I don't want anybody in the media to take any offense, but sometimes they're right, sometimes they're not right. So –

MR. SIMPSON: I can agree with that.

MR. GOWDY: So in this instance, we can all celebrate the fact that they were correct. You were hired by the Washington Free Beacon?

MR. SIMPSON: That was the client, yes.

MR. GOWDY: All right. And what were your instructions? What were you asked to do?

MR. SIMPSON: I -- that's I think covered - our client relationships are confidential, and so I can't get into what anyone specifically told me.

I think I can speak more broadly and say that it (The Free Beacon engagement) was an open-ended look at Donald Trump's business career

and his litigation history and his relationships with questionable people, how much he was really worth, how he ran his casinos, what kind of performance he had in other lines of work. It was a very broad unfocused look, which is the way we do our business...

And only after you've digested all that information do you start to figure out, you know, where to focus your inquiries.

MR. GOWDY: Were you asked to write a report or just accumulate information?

MR. SIMPSON: Again, I need to steer clear of specific communications I had with my clients, but I can tell you that as a business practice, generally speaking, we do engagements on a 30-day basis, and at the end of the 30 days we write a report about what we found. And if there's specific things that are interesting, a particular lawsuit or a dispute or a business deal or something like that, you know, we will write a separate treatment of that issue. But, generally speaking, for most of our clients, particularly in the beginning of an engagement, it's a 30-day assignment, and at the end of 30 days you get a report. And if you think what we told you was interesting and you want more, we can sign up again.

MR. GOWDY: Well, I really am trying to limit the number of times your lawyer has to lean over there and give you counsel, so I'm trying to stay within the parameters of what I think you feel like you're able to answer. But are you asked to write what some of our friends may refer to as a fair and balanced piece, or are they primarily interested in negative information?

MR. SIMPSON: Well, we've only had a very small number of political clients. So I can tell you, I mean, our methodology doesn't really change. We - my firm is -- all the principals are former journalists, so we don't come out of the political combat industry.

We come out of the, you know, journalism industry, which is all about sort of sticking to the facts and not leaping to conclusions and not trying to, you know, come up with a hit piece on anybody.

So, generally speaking, what we get compensated for is producing reliable treatments of whatever the subject is. And I should just add, I mean, it doesn't - it doesn't help us or our clients if we only look for negative information. What the clients want is all the information.

And so, you know, someone -- if you're in a campaign and the, you know, other side is a businessman and you're reviewing his career, it's important information whether he's a good businessman or bad businessman. And you don't want your client trying to make an issue of his business career if he's a brilliant businessman who knows how to make money in an honest and ethical way.

===
BACK TO SENATE EXAM WITH MS. SAWYER

WHAT DID FUSION GPS DO FOR "FREE BEACON"?

MS. SAWYER

Q: And are you free today to talk to us about any of the actual findings from that research and that engagement (Free Beacon)?

A: Yes.

Q: Okay. So with regard to that initial engagement because you had talked a bit about some of the research you had done -- I think you said it was holistic, financials, potential ties to organized crime.
With regard to this initial engagement that started in October, September, can you just explain for us what your findings were?

A: I guess I'll just give you the caveat that, you know, it's a group effort. So I can tell you, you know, as the person that was, you know, running the project, you know, I had my fingers in various things, but there were also the things that I was directly focused on.

In the early -- the very first weekend that I started boning up on Donald Trump, you know, I found various references to him having connections to Italian organized crime and later to a Russian organized crime figure named Felix Sater, S-A-T-E-R.

It wasn't hard to find, it wasn't any great achievement, it was in *the New York Times*, but as someone who has done a lot of Russian organized crime investigations as a journalist, originally that caught my attention and became something that I focused on while other people looked at other things.

So from the very beginning of this organized crime was -- Russian organized crime was a focus of interest.

I guess I should just repeat, you know, this is a subject that I covered extensively at the Wall Street Journal. I wrote a series of front-page articles about various corrupt politicians from Russia, oligarchs, and one of the things that I wrote about was the connections between western politicians and Russian business figures.

I was sort of an amateur student of the subject (Russian mafia) and I had written about some of these same Russian crime figures, you know, years earlier in the U.S. and various frauds and things they were involved in.

As it happens, Felix Sater was, you know, connected to the same Russian crime family that was at issue in the Prevezon case (a Fusion GPS Russian case), which is the dominant Russian crime family in Russia and has a robust U.S. presence and is involved in a lot of crime and criminal activity in the United

For the Forgotten Americans

States and for many years was the -- the leader of this family was on the FBI most wanted list and lives openly in Moscow as a fugitive from U.S. law for a very elaborate stock fraud.

Q: Who is that individual and family?

A: The first name is Semyon, S-E-M-Y-O-N, the last name is Mogilevich, M-O-G-I-L-E-V-I-C-H.Mogilevich is sometimes referred to as the "Brainy Don" because he runs very sophisticated schemes including, according to the FBI, involving natural gas pipelines in Europe, and he's wanted in connection with an elaborate stock fraud called "YBM Magnex" that was took place in the Philadelphia area. **You know, Russian organized crime is very different from Italian organized crime.**

It's much more sort of a hybrid kind of thing where they're (Russian) involved in politics and banking and there's even a lot of connections between the mafia and the KGB or the FSB and cyber-crime, things that the Italians sort of never figured out. Stock fraud in particular was the big thing in the U.S.In any event, all of that entered into my thinking when I saw that Donald Trump was in business with Felix Sater in the "Trump SOHO" project and a number of other controversial condo projects.

Q: What, if anything, did you conclude about the connection between and in the business dealings that then Candidate Trump had had with Mr. Sater?

A: Well, somewhat analogous to the Browder situation (also Prevezon). I found it notable this was something he (Trump) didn't want to talk about and testified under oath he wouldn't know Felix if he ran into him in the street. **That was not true. He (Trump) knew him (Sater) well and, in fact, continued to associate with him long after he learned of Felix's organized crime ties.**

So, you know, that tells you something about somebody. So I concluded that he was okay with that and that was a troubling thing. I also, you know, began to -- I keep saying I, but we as a company began to look at where his (Trump's) money came from and, you know, that raised a lot of questions.

We saw indications that some of the (Trump) money came from Kazakhstan, among other places, and that some of it you just couldn't account for.

You know, we also conducted a much broader sort of look at his entire career and his overseas investments in places like Europe and Latin America. You know, it wasn't really a Russia focused investigation for the first half of it.

That was just one component of a broader look at his business career

We spent a lot of time trying to figure out whether he's (Trumps') really as rich as he says he is because that was the subject of a libel case that he filed against a journalist named Tim O'Brien for which there was quite a lot of discovery and litigation filings detailing O'Brien's allegation that he was worth, you know, maybe a fifth to a third of what he claims and Trump's angry retort that he was worth far more than that.

We looked at the golf courses and whether they actually ever made any money and how much debt they had.

We looked at the bankruptcies, how could somebody go through so many bankruptcies, you know, and still have a billion dollars in personal assets.

So those are the kinds of things.

We looked at a lot of things like his tax bills. Tax bills are useful because you can figure out how much money someone is making or how much they're worth or how much their properties are worth based on how much they have to pay in taxes.

One of the things we found out was that, you know, when it comes to paying taxes, Donald Trump claims to not have much stuff. At least the Trump organization. So they would make filings with various state and local authorities saying that their buildings weren't worth much.

Q: And this information that you gathered, was it shared with the client that you had for that September, October engagement?

A: I can't answer that.

MS. QUINT: [Lara Quint, Chief Counsel, Democrat Senator Whitehouse]:

When you said you looked at the golf courses and bankruptcies, just to clarify, everything you're talking about was for that 2015. When you say it wasn't Russia focused at first, I'm unclear of the time.

MS. SAWYER: Yeah. Can you tell us when that engagement ended?

MR. LEVY: Which question is pending? Can you repeat the question?

MS. QUINT: I think they're related. I lost track when you said you looked at golf courses, bankruptcies, tax bills and it was not initially Russia centric. I'm wondering the time frame to make sure we're all on the same page.

MR. SIMPSON: It's difficult to specifically recall when we did exactly what. For example, the specific issue of the golf courses I think did come up later, much later, but these things run in stages.

For instance, in the early stage of an investigation, you know, particularly of Donald Trump you want to get every lawsuit the guy's ever been in. **So, you know, we collected lawsuits from around the country and the world.**

And I do remember one of the earlier things we did was we collected a lot of documents from **Scotland** because he'd been in a big controversy there about land use. There had been another one in **Ireland**.

There was a lot of Freedom of Information Act requests and that sort of thing. So in the early phases of something you're collecting lots of paper on every subject imaginable.

So in the course of reading that litigation we would follow up on things that were interesting, such as a libel case against a journalist that he settled, which, in other words, he didn't prevail in his attempts to prove he was a billionaire.

BY MS. SAWYER:

Q: So one way to help clarify this is just to -- you know, we had been talking about an engagement that began in September or October of 2015. Can you tell us when that particular engagement ended?

A: I can only estimate it.

Q: And in general when do you think that ended?

A: Spring of 2016.

MR. LEVY: Don't guess.

MR. SIMPSON: I'm sorry.

BY MS. SAWYER:

Q: Okay. But that engagement did come to an end and it came to an end before November 8th, the election, November 8, 2016?

A: It did end before the election, yes.

Q: Then did you continue doing opposition work on Candidate Trump -- then Candidate Trump, now President Trump for a different client?

A: Yes.

Q: And can you tell us generally when that engagement began?

A: It was in the first half of 2016.

Q: And what, if anything, can you tell us about that client?

A: Nothing.

MR. LEVY: Not nothing as a factual matter, but he's going to decline to answer that question.

MS. SAWYER: And the basis again for declining that question?

MR. LEVY: Privilege.

MS. SAWYER: Okay.

MR. LEVY: And other obligations of confidentiality.

MS. SAWYER: Just to be clear for the record, specifically what privilege?

MR. LEVY: The privileges that we previously asserted with the committee. They're in our April 7 and June 23 letters.

MS. SAWYER: Okay.

Q: With regard to the engagements, both of these engagements to do opposition research on Candidate Trump, were you paid directly by each of the clients or was there an intermediary paying you?

A: I think I'd like to confer with my lawyer about this.

MR. LEVY: Sure.

(Whereupon a discussion was had sotto voce.)

MR. SIMPSON: I'm going to decline to answer that question.

MS. SAWYER: And, again, the grounds for declining?

MR. LEVY: It's a voluntary interview and it would implicate privileges and obligations that we've set forth with the committee potentially.

MS. SAWYER: Sure.

===

ENTER PERKINS COIE

CRITICAL INSERT from HPSCI: During Simpson's Senate examination, he refused to mention that **the law firm of Perkins Coie was the second client.**

> [NOTE: Wikipedia states that: *Perkins Coie is counsel of record for the Democratic National Committee, Democratic Leadership Council, the Democratic Senatorial Campaign Committee, and the Democratic Congressional Campaign Committee. It has also represented several presidential campaigns, , Barack Obama, and Hillary Clinton.[*

MR. GOWDY: How long were you employed by The Washington Free Beacon?

MR. SIMPSON: As I said, I think we started in September or October, and I think it wound down in April, sometime in the spring. As the Republican primaries came to an end, it became obvious that that work was going to end.

MR. GOWDY: Did you rely on sources or sub-sources during your work for the Washington Free Beacon?

MR. SIMPSON: I don't specifically remember. We may have engaged someone. Typically speaking, we engage subcontractors to gather documents in faraway places. And, you know, far away in this case may be even just being California or Illinois or something like that. So I assume we had some subcontractors, for instance, but I don't specifically remember.

MR. GOWDY: At some point, did the Free Beacon stop paying you for the project into then-candidate Trump? Did the business relationship end?

MR. SIMPSON: I remember that we stopped doing the Trump work for "The Beacon" sometime in the spring of 2016.

MR. GOWDY: Did you pick up –

MR. SIMPSON: I don't know the exact date of when the payments... So I can tell you more substantively when it stopped, but I don't - you know, the records are not something that I'm immersed in.

MR. GOWDY: Well, let's go with that. When did the work stop?

MR. SIMPSON: I think it was April or May.

MR. GOWDY: All right. And were you retained by a subsequent client to pick up on the work that you had begun?

MR. SIMPSON: It was the same subject. And obviously, the first work was informed by the new project. But, you know, it wasn't like a direct line continuum. It was similar work, but we obviously by then knew quite a bit about Mr. Trump and his business career and his associations and all that.

MR. GOWDY: Did you have a second client interested in opposition research on candidate Trump?

MR. SIMPSON: Yes, sir.

MR. GOWDY: Who was that second client?

MR. SIMPSON: I think the records indicated that it's Perkins Coie and I can confirm that.

MR. GOWDY: And who is Perkins Coie?

MR. SIMPSON: It's a law firm. I think they're headquartered in Seattle and they're a big law firm.

MR. GOWDY: Had you ever worked for them in the past?

MR. SIMPSON: -- I haven't been released by any clients to get into my work for them. Generally speaking, we sign confidentiality agreements with all of our clients, which is an essential part of the kind of work we do. And I haven't been released or directed to get into whether I worked for these clients before or what kind of things I did for them.

MR. GOWDY: So I assume you did not sign a confidentiality agreement with the Washington Free Beacon?

MR. SIMPSON: I mean, my answer for the second client (Perkins Coie) would be the same as my answer for the first, which is that I worked for *The Wall Street Journal* for about 15 years, and I specialized in complex financial investigations, political corruption, that sort of thing...

MR. GOWDY: Well, let's try to approach it this way. When you were hired by Perkins Coie, did you consider them to be the client?

MR. SIMPSON: Yes.

MR. GOWDY: Do you recall who, if anyone, you specifically talked to at Perkins Coie?

MR. SIMPSON: I think that would be getting into client communication.

MR. GOWDY: All right. We'll keep trying...Were you aware that Perkins Coie was retained by the DNC?

MR. SIMPSON: I'm aware. I was aware of that and have been for years that they have -- they were one of the main lawyers for the Democratic party, yes. I don't have any specific awareness –

MR. GOWDY: That wasn't my precise question. With respect to this fact pattern, with respect to your firm being retained, were you aware that Perkins Coie was working on behalf of the DNC?

MR. SIMPSON: Yes. I mean, I know that they are - the DNC is a client of Perkins Coie. I don't - I didn't see it -- nobody gave me a document or informed me specifically of that.

MR. GOWDY: Did you think the firm was just doing it on their own?

MR. SIMPSON: I'm sorry. I don't understand your question.

MR. GOWDY: Did you think the firm was just doing it on their own?

MR. SIMPSON: Doing what? Doing –

MR. GOWDY: Opposition research into candidate Trump.

MR. SIMPSON: No.

MR. GOWDY: Paying you to do opposition research into candidate Trump. Did you think Perkins Coie was doing that on their own?

MR. SIMPSON: No, sir. What I'm trying to explain is that I have been in Washington for several decades, and I spent a lot of time on Capitol Hill and it was well-known to me that Perkins Coie represents the DNC.

MR. GOWDY: Is that the only way you knew they were doing work on behalf of the DNC when they retained you in this specific fact pattern?

MR. SIMPSON: I'm not sure I understand what you're trying to ask me, but if it's - I'm not going to get into what discussions I had with my client about who their clients were.

MR. GOWDY: I'm looking at a release from Perkins Coie that is giving me more information than you are. Have you seen the release where they released you from some of your confidentiality obligations?

MR. SIMPSON: I would like to see a copy of that, if you don't mind.

MR. GOWDY: Do your lawyers not have it?

MR. SIMPSON: It's been a busy time. Okay. Okay. I'm sorry if I'm not giving you a clear answer. **I knew it was the DNC that we were working for.**

MR. GOWDY: Okay. How did you know it was the DNC?

MR. SIMPSON: I honestly don't -- I couldn't tell you if someone specifically said this is for the DNC... I feel like I'm in a difficult position, because I have not been released from my client - by my client to talk about anything that we talked about, but I'm trying to give you the answer that I think you want, which is I was definitely aware that Perkins Coie represented the DNC and that they were the client in this matter.

MR. GOWDY: Right. And I'm asking you how you knew that?

For the Forgotten Americans

MR. SIMPSON: And I'm -- I don't know what to tell you other than that I was generally aware that Perkins Coie represented the DNC.

MR. GOWDY: Okay. So how did your work for Perkins Coie begin?

MR. SIMPSON: My recollection is we began to review what we had learned over the previous months and talk about what we would do, you know, now that we would have resources to pursue this - some of these matters further.

So it's -- when you get into that point of a piece of research, you begin to develop lines of inquiry and things that you think might be important, things you want to -- that other people are - you know other people are interested in. So we began to develop more specific lines of inquiry.

So they -- so the things that we started looking at specifically were a lot of Mr. Trump's overseas business deals, his history with regard to tax disputes.

We were very interested in things like his clothing line ... while he was running on a platform of economic nationalism that he's outsourced his clothing line to developing countries.

So we were interested in the labor practices around his factories. You know, we had gradually accumulated more and more things about his bankruptcies. And we had gotten a better sense of who his business partners were. So those were issues. When we reached an agreement about, you know, funding and we thought we would have funding to do a bunch of things, **we began to look for people who could help us pursue some of these things.**

MR. GOWDY: Were the lines of inquiry dictated by the client or suggested by the client, or did you come up with those on your own?

MR. SIMPSON: Generally speaking, we seek and usually receive a lot of leeway to develop our lines of inquiry. ...So we like to get -- we like to have a lot of freedom to pursue everything or the things that we think are important, because we have found from experience that clients, you know, generally they have something that they maybe are trying to do or have some preconceived notions about things, and we find that to be unhelpful..

MR. GOWDY: What was the budget for you to enjoy the freedom to pursue the lines of inquiry you wanted to pursue?

MR. SIMPSON: I don't remember being given a specific expenses budget. I think the fees were $50,000 a month.

MR. GOWDY: Flat fee, $50,000 a month?

MR. SIMPSON: That's right.

MR. GOWDY: Plus expenses, minus expenses?

MR. SIMPSON: Plus expenses, yes.

CHAPTER 16

CHRISTOPHER STEELE

SIMPSON SAYS

You know, in the background of ALL international business is questions about corruption.

The Trump organization had branched out all over the world in like the four to eight years prior to 2016.

-- it was opaque what Donald Trump had been doing on these business trips to Russia. We didn't know what he was doing there.

So by its very nature the question of whether something is accurate isn't really asked.
The question that is asked generally is whether it's credible. Human intelligence isn't good for, you know, filing lawsuits.

You don't really decide who's telling the truth.
You decide whether the person is credible, right, whether they know what they're talking about...

WHO IS CHRISTOPHER STEELE
WHY WAS HE HIRED BY FUSION GPS?

BACK TO THE SENATE EXAM BY MS. SAWYER

Q: It has been widely reported that you engaged Christopher Steele to do part of the research, the opposition research on Candidate Trump. Is that accurate?

A: Yes.

Q: And he was working in that capacity as a subcontractor for you? And when I say "you" here I mean Fusion GPS.

A: Yes.

Q: And when did you engage Mr. Steele to conduct opposition research on Candidate Trump?

A: I don't specifically recall, but it would have been in the -- it would have been **May or June of 2016**.

Q: And why did you engage Mr. Steele in May or June of 2016?

A: **That calls for a somewhat long answer.** We had done an enormous amount of work on Donald Trump generally at this point in the project and we began to drill down on specific areas.

He was not the only subcontractor that we engaged. Other parts of the world required other people. For example, we were interested in the fact that the Trump family was selling merchandise under the Trump brand in the United States that was made in sweat shops in Asia and South America -- or Latin America. So we needed someone else for that. So there were other things.

We were not totally focused on Russia at that time (Free Beacon engagement), but we were at a point where we were -- you know, we'd done a lot of reading and research and we were drilling down on specific areas. Scotland was another one. So that's the answer.

What happens when you get to this point in an investigation when you've gathered all of the public record information and you've begun to exhaust your open source, you know, resources is that you tend to find specialists who can take you further into a subject.

And I had known Chris since I left the Wall Street Journal.

He was the lead Russianist at MI6 prior to leaving the government and an extremely well-regarded investigator, researcher, and, as I say, we're friends and share interest in Russian kleptocracy and organized crime issues. I would say that's broadly why I asked him to see what he could find out about Donald Trump's business activities in Russia.

Q: So in May or June 2016 you hired Christopher Steele to, as you've just indicated, find out what he could about Donald Trump's business activities in

Russia. <u>Did something in trigger that assignment</u>?

A: No, I don't think I could point to something in particular as a trigger.

I mean, the basis for the (Steele) request (was he (Trump) had made a number of trips to Russia and talked about doing a number of business deals but never did one, and that struck me as a little bit odd and calling for an explanation. You know, in the background of ALL international business is questions about corruption. The Trump organization had branched out all over the world in like the four to eight years prior to 2016.

So in any kind of investigation you would naturally want to know whether there was some issue with improper business relationships. I'll just stress that we weren't looking for -- at least it wasn't at the forefront of my mind there was going to be anything involving the Russian government per se, at least not that I recall.

Q: So at the time you first hired him (Steele) had it been publicly reported that there had been a cyber-intrusion into the Democratic National Convention computer system?

A: I don't specifically remember.

What I know was that there was chatter around Washington about hacking of the Democrats and Democratic think tanks and other things like that and there was a site that had sprung up called D.C. Leaks that seemed to suggest that somebody was up to something. I don't think at the time at least that we were particularly focused on -- well, I don't specifically remember.

Q: So you hired Mr. Steele. Had you worked with him before?

A: Yes.

Q: And can you generally describe what he had done in the capacity of working with you and your firm, what kind of projects?

A: Generally speaking, like me, Chris tends to work for lawyers who are attempting to assist clients in litigation or an asset recovery-type situation.

And so, you know, the former Soviet Union throws off an enormous number of disputes about who owns what because of the history of state ownership of everything and the transfers of property into private hands following the collapse of the Soviet Union was a murky process.

So particularly in Europe there's a lot of disputes over who really owns what. And so we would collaborate on those kinds of investigations.

Sometimes a controversy would spill over into the United States and, you know, I would be asked to see if I could find a company here or there or run director searches on individuals who might be associated with people we were interested in, that sort of thing. It's interesting work, but it's kind of plain vanilla business intelligence, litigation support stuff.

Q: And roughly how many years -- over how many years, like when do you first recall working with him?

A: I believe we met in 2009. We've worked together since 2009.

Q: How did you find the quality of his work over that period of time?

A: Quality is a really important issue in the business intelligence industry. There's a lot of poor quality work and a lot of people make a lot of promises about what they can do and who they know and what they can find out. Then there's a lot of people who operate in sort of improper questionable ways.

Chris was, you know, a person who delivered quality work in very appropriate ways. So -- I hope you won't be insulted, but he's basically a Boy Scout.

You know, he worked for the government for a very long time. He lives a very modest, quiet life, and, you know, this is his specialty. We got along very well because my specialty is public information. So he was comfortable working with me and I was comfortable working with him and, you know, we've both been around a lot of criminal investigations and national security stuff.....

Q: Specific to the engagement with regard to research on Candidate Trump, why did you specifically ask Mr. Steele to do that work?

A: The way our firm runs we pursue things, you know, somewhat out of curiosity. So we didn't know -- **it was opaque what Donald Trump had been doing on these business trips to Russia. We didn't know what he was doing there.** So I gave Chris --we gave Chris a sort of assignment that would be typical for us which was pretty open ended. We said see if you can find out what Donald Trump's been doing on these trips to Russia.

Since Chris and I worked together over the years there's a lot that didn't need to be said. That would include who is he doing business with, which hotels does he like to stay at, you know, did anyone ever offer him anything, you know, the standard sort of things you would look at. I don't think I gave him any specific instructions beyond the general find out what he was up to.

Q: Did you engage anyone else to do that particular research?

A: In Russia?

Q: Yes.

A: So we had other people like Ed Baumgartner who, you know, by this time -- I guess Prevezon was still winding down, but who would do Russian language research which didn't involve going to Russia. It just involves reading Russian newspaper accounts and that sort of thing.

Q: So was Mr. Baumgartner also working on opposition research for Trump?

A: At some point, I think probably after the end of the Prevezon case we asked him to help with I think -- my specific recollection is he **worked on specific issues involving Paul Manafort and Ukraine.**

Q: With regard to the presidential election of 2016?

A: Yes.

Q: We had talked about work for multiple clients. What steps were taken, if any, to make sure that the work that Mr. Baumgartner was doing for Prevezon was not shared across to the clients you were working for with regard to the presidential election?

A: He didn't deal with them. He didn't deal with clients. There wouldn't have been any reason to -- he operates under the same rules that I do.

Q: And with regard to Mr. Steele, did he ever do any work for Fusion GPS on the Prevezon litigation matter?

A: No.

Q: It's my understanding that Mr. Steele works with a company called Orbis & Associates. Did anyone else at Orbis, to the best of your knowledge, work with Mr. Steele on the engagement that you had with him related to Cand. Trump?

A: I mean, I don't know their names.

Q: So do you know whether anyone else worked with him?

A: Yes. I mean, do you mean as subcontractors or within his company?

Q: First within his company.

MR. LEVY: If you know.

BY THE WITNESS [SIMPSON]:

A: I just don't remember their names. I remember meeting somebody in London who I think worked on it, but I just don't remember.

Q: Somebody else associated with Orbis?

A: Yes.

Q: With regard to the assignment that you gave to Mr. Steele to do Russia-related research for Candidate Trump, is that an accurate way to describe it? I said Russia-related research with regard to Candidate Trump. Would that be a fair way to describe the assignment?

A: Yes.

Q: Did you have any input into the actual work that he did? Did you give him directions as to what to research specifically?

A: I don't recall giving him specific instructions.

We spoke on the phone about various areas of interest. For example, when Paul Manafort was elevated to running the campaign, we talked about Paul Manafort and his long history of dealings with Russian oligarchs. So it's more of a collaboration than, you know, sort of manager-employee kind of relationship. You know, we would talk about things that were interesting to us and that seemed to be -- you know, needed to be (indecipherable).

Q: So is it fair to describe it as you would collaboratively discuss potential topics to explore?

A: Yes, I think that's fair.

Q: And did you conduct any of the actual research yourself?

A: Well, I think it's important to understand we were doing in my company, you know, all kinds of research, including lots of Russia research, and part of what you do when you get information from someone outside the company who's specifically looking at a discrete set of questions or issues is you add it to the stuff you've already gathered.

So we did all kinds of stuff on public information about Donald Trump's business trips to Russia and business dealings with Russians.

I mean, Chris's role was specifically to do the thing that we couldn't do, which was to arrange to talk to people. Generally speaking, we don't do a lot of interviewing. Our research is very document focused.

Q: So to the extent you can describe, when you say he (Steele) was doing something you could not do and that was he was arranging to talk to people,

can you describe who it was he (Steele) was reaching out to, what you knew about that?

A: I don't think for security reasons, among other things, it's an area I'm not going to be able to go into in terms of sources and things like that.

I think speaking broadly, you know, there's a large diaspora of Russians around the world and people in Moscow that, you know, are talking to each other all the time.

The thing that people forget about what was going on in June of 2016 was that no one was really focused on sort of this question of whether Donald Trump had a relationship with the Kremlin. So, you know, when Chris started asking around in Moscow about this the information was sitting there. It wasn't a giant secret. People were talking about it freely.

It was only, you know, later that it became a subject of great controversy and people clammed up, and at that time the whole issue of the hacking was also, you know, not really focused on Russia. So these things eventually converged into, you know, a major issue, but at the time it wasn't one.

Q: I have five or so more minutes and I have a lot more questions just about some of that work, but I do want to just pin down a couple things about the engagement in particular before we end this hour.

So with regard to selecting Mr. Steele specifically to do the Russia -- to do work on Candidate Trump's ties to Russia, do you believe based on his experience and background that

Mr. Steele would have been aware of the potential in his discussions with these people that he could be fed this information?

A: When Chris -- I don't believe it, I know it.

When Chris briefs in a sort of more formal setting, which I've seen, you know, when he introduces himself -- you know, he was the lead Russianist for MI6.

So the first sort of beginning of that is he says, you know, I've worked on this issue all my life and when you're trained in Russian intelligence matters the fundamental problem of your profession is disinformation. It's the number one issue. In any collection of field -- you know, information from the field you should assume that there will be possibly some disinformation and that, you know, as a professional who has dedicated my life to this, you know, I am trained to spot possible or likely disinformation. So it's front and center when you gather information in Russia.

Q: And when you hired him to do the work, did the client -- were you still working for -- at any time did you work for two clients on this opposition research? Did they overlap, the two clients?

A: I just don't know. I can just tell you that it was -- I mean, things follow the political cycle.

So there was a point at which the Republican primaries were fundamentally over and the Democrats hadn't really begun yet. So there was some transition period. That's all I can say. I don't keep the books at my place. So I would feel -- I'm afraid to give you a wrong answer that. I just don't know.

Q: Did either client know that you had hired Mr. Steele specifically?

A: I don't think I can answer that.

Q: And on what basis can you not answer that?

MR. LEVY: The answer to that question would -- could require the disclosure of client communications which might implicate privileges and obligations that we've previously set forth to the committee.

BY MS. SAWYER:

Q: Okay. Maybe you can answer this question, then.

Did either client ever direct Mr. Steele themselves, directly engage and have conversations with Mr. Steele?

A: I don't think I can answer that.

MR. LEVY: Do you want to take a break?

MR. SIMPSON: Sure.

===

MORE ON THE SIMPSON-STEELE RELATIONSHIP

MR. GOWDY: How did he come to work on this?

For the Forgotten Americans

MR. SIMPSON: As I said, I mean, we've done other things together. And over - well, at the very beginning of this project, one of the very first things that I focused on was Donald Trump's relationship with a convicted racketeer named Felix Sater, and who was alleged to have an organized crime, Russian organized crime background.

And over the course of the first phase of this or the first project, we developed a lot of additional information suggesting that the company that Donald Trump had been associated with and Felix Sater, Bayrock, was engaged in illicit financial business activity and had organized crime connections. **We also had sort of more broadly <u>learned</u> that Mr. Trump had long time associations with Italian organized crime figures.**

And as we pieced together the early years of his (Trump's) biography, it seemed as if during the early part of his career he **(Trump) had connections to a lot of Italian mafia figures, and then gradually during the nineties became associated with Russian mafia figures**.

And so all of that had developed by the spring of 2016 to the point where it was not a speculative piece of research; **it was pretty well-established.** And Mr. Trump had, quite memorably, attempted to downplay his relationship with Mr. Sater in ways that I found, frankly, suspicious and not credible. Saying he wouldn't recognize him on the street, but there were pictures of them together.

And the other people around Bayrock were also from the former Soviet Union and also had associations suggestive of possible organized crime ties. One of them is a guy named Tevfik Arif, who it turned out his real name was Tofik Arifov, and that he was an alleged organized crime figure from the central Asia. So there was all that.

And then, you know, we also increasingly saw that Mr. Trump's business career had evolved over the prior decade into a lot of projects in overseas places, particularly in the former Soviet Union, that were very opaque, and that **he (Trump) had made a number of trips to Russia, but said he'd never done a business deal there. And I found that mysterious.**

And so I had the perfect person to go see if they could figure out what was going on there. And so that's how I decided to ask Chris if he could look into it for me.

And I had - the initial engagement with Chris was much like we do. I didn't hire him for a long-term engagement. I said, take 30 days, 20 or 30 days,· and we'll pay you a set amount of money, and see if you can figure out what Trump's been up to over there, because he's gone over (to Russia) a bunch of times, he (Trump) said some weird things about Putin, but doesn't seem to have gotten any business deals.

MR. GOWDY: <u>And how much did you pay Chris Steele?</u>

MR. SIMPSON: I think what we've told the committee from the bank records is that it was ultimately $160,000. That sounds right to me. I think probably the initial engagement was for 20 or 30 thousand dollars. There's, you know, currency differences between pounds and dollars, so I don't remember how it was denominated or exactly how it was priced.

MR. GOWDY: Now, help me understand this. Would that payment for Steele have been expensed to the law firm, or would Fusion have paid that out of its own money that it received from the law firm?

MR. SIMPSON: I believe, at least if things were running the way I hope they ran, it was expensed to the law firm.

MR. GOWDY: So Perkins Coie paid Chris Steele?

MR. SIMPSON: I think it was, I mean, I think we billed them for it.

MR. GOWDY: Okay.

MR. SIMPSON: I was generally aware of Chris' history. You know, because of the strictures on government work, when you're involved in intelligence and talking about it, we never discussed in any great detail what kind of work he did. And at least publicly it was - even though he had been exposed in a prior leak by a former government agent over there, so it was, in fact, in the public domain that he had worked for British Intelligence. He generally didn't talk about his government work other than the way you would if you formerly worked for the government. I used to work for the government, you know. Sometimes he would say foreign office. But we had mutual friends who were familiar with his background.

MR. SCHIFF: Just to clarify, Mr. Gowdy, you're not confirming or denying, you're just asking?

MR. GOWDY: I'm just asking what he said.

MR. GOWDY: Did you ever have any conversations with the FBI?

MR. SIMPSON: Not about this, no.

SIMPSON SAYS:
STEELE NEVER WENT TO RUSSIA

MR. GOWDY: Did Chris Steele go to Russia as part of this project?

MR. SIMPSON: No, sir.

MR. GOWDY: How do you know that?

MR. SIMPSON: Well, that's what he told me. I mean, assuming - unless it was a covert thing that he was keeping from his client, he would have billed me for it.

MR. GOWDY: <u>How was he able to accumulate information in Russia if he didn't go?</u>

MR. SIMPSON: Well, so to be clear, he really would not be safe if he went to Russia. He's been exposed as a former undercover British Intelligence officer who worked in Moscow. So it wouldn't be wise for him to go to Russia. So, to answer your question, you know, generally speaking, his line of work is very different from mine and that was why I hired him.

So I do mostly public records and we don't do much interviewing. But I'm familiar with how his work is done.

And generally, you have a network of sources who live in or came from the place that you're interested in. So, you know, generally speaking, you would have -- you would run a network of Sub-Sources or subcontractors who travel around and gather information for you. And so without getting into who his sources are, I can say generally, he (Steele) hires people who can travel and talk to people and find out what's going on.

==

BACK TO THE SENATE EXAM BY MS. SAWYER:

SIMPSON SAYS:
ACCURACY ISN'T ASKED

MS. SAWYER: I think the question pending was just whether or not the clients specifically spoke with or directed Mr. Steele's work?

MR. LEVY: So he can't talk about client communications, directions to the client -- directions to Mr. Steele as those communications might implicate privilege or obligations.

BY MS. SAWYER:

All right. So we'll get to that. We'll talk about that a little bit later...

Q: And you had talked a bit about prior work and Mr. Steele's performance in prior work and being satisfied by that work.

<u>Did you do anything to kind of test and make sure that information he (Steele) was giving you was accurate?</u>

A: -- I know I'm repeating myself, but generally we do public records work. So we deal in documents and things that are very hard and that are useful in court or, you know, other kinds of proceedings. Chris deals in a very different kind of information, which is human intelligence, human information.

So by its very nature the question of whether something is accurate isn't really asked. The question that is asked generally is whether it's credible. Human intelligence isn't good for, you know, filing lawsuits.

And it's good for making decisions and trying to understand what's going on and that's a really valuable thing, but it's not the same thing.So when you evaluate human intelligence, human reporting, field reporting, source reporting, you know, it's sort of like when you're a journalist and you're trying to figure out who's telling the truth, right.

You don't really decide who's telling the truth. You decide whether the person is credible, right, whether they know what they're talking about, whether there's other reasons to believe what they're saying, whether anything they've said factually matches up with something in the public record.

So, you know, we would evaluate his memos based on whether he told us something we didn't know from somewhere else that we were then able to run down. So, you know, for example, he, you know, wrote a memo about a Trump campaign advisor named Carter Page and his mysterious trip to Moscow.

Q: I'm just going to stop you for a moment because I hadn't yet gotten to the specific stuff of the Trump assignment. I was just trying to get a sense of the specific ways in which you assessed his performance in determining to hire him.

A: That's how we did it. We would assess it based on the content and the credibility of -- we'd try to determine the credibility of what we were reading.

MR. MUSE: His reference was to give you an example. I think that's where he was going.

MR. SIMPSON: Yeah.

MS. SAWYER: I understand and I appreciate that and we'll get to that. I just didn't want to -- in light of the time I didn't want to get you started down that road. If I could just have a second because I want to make sure we finish our questions on this topic and we'll resume our next hour with some of the others.

MR. SIMPSON: Okay.

MS. SAWYER: So we'll go off the record. It's high noon, 12:00. So let's go off the record. (A short break was had.)

BY MR. DAVIS [Deputy Chief Investigative Counsel for Chairman Grassley]: We're back on the record. It's 12:06 p.m.

[**NOTE:** Mr. Davis spends about an hour on the Prevezon subject. In order to focus on the Steele Dossier, I will refer this for later].

CHAPTER 17

THE STEELE DOSSIER

SIMPSON SAYS

it was not particularly useful for the kind of things that are, you know, useful in politics, which are things that you can prove, things that you can say, things that people will believe.

a Russian oligarch having a meeting with Senator John McCain shortly before the 2008 presidential election

he (Steele) said don't worry about that, I know the perfect (FBI) person, I have a contact there, they'll listen to me, they know who I am, I'll take care of it

MS. SAWYER: Chief Oversight Counsel, Senator Feinstein:
So this particular memo (of the Steele Dossier) that we've been talking about, this first one doesn't specifically mention, as far as I can see, any efforts to interfere by Russia.

INSIDE THE STEELE DOSSIER

IT'S 1:55. SENATE EXAMINATION RESUMES BY MS. SAWYER:

Q: I'm going to return you back to discussing the work at Fusion that Christopher Steele had done during the Presidential election of 2016. It has been widely reported and Mr. Steele has acknowledged that he created 16 memos before the election between the time period of June of 2016 and October of 2016. Is that accurate?

A: To the best of my knowledge, that's accurate.

Q: And he also has acknowledged -- Mr. Steele also has acknowledged and it's been reported that there was one additional memo that came after the election in December of 2016. Is that also accurate?

A: I think what he has said is that -- yeah, that's basically accurate. What he said was that the series of memos that were published by *BuzzFeed*, that's the package (Steele Dossier) that you're talking about.

Q: And so I'm going to show you what we will just mark as Exhibit 3 for identification purposes. So Exhibit 3 that I've just given you is a document that was produced to the committee by your lawyers, and they had explained to us that this was a document originally posted by *BuzzFeed* in January of 2017 and it has Bates numbers down in the right-hand corner.

The first one is CLMS-JC-00041391 and then the last one is number 41425. If you could just take a look at that. Is that what we were just discussing as the series of memos posted by ***BuzzFeed*** and created by Mr. Steele?

A: Yes, it is.

Q: Can you explain for us just what – does this represent the 16 memos that would have occurred between June and October of 2016 that Mr. Steele created?

A: These are the memos that he created under the engagement and then this extra one that is appended. I never actually numbered – totaled them up, but these are the ones I'm familiar with.

Q: And does this represent the entire universe of memos that Mr. Steele created as part of this particular engagement for you?

A: To the best of my knowledge as part of this engagement, this is it.

Q: And can you just explain to us so that we understand the document, it has a heading "Company Intelligence Report." I'm just looking at the first page. That one says "Company Intelligence Report 2016/080." What would that have signified?

A: Company Intelligence Report is just a way of saying it's not a government document.

In the event that, you know, someone stole it or it leaked or there was some sort of breach, you know, they're not going to have their own name on it, but they want to make sure that no one mistakes it for a government document. That's my understanding.

"080" is their internal numbering system for, you know, their production of memoranda, and the reason it jumps from 80 to 86 is -- I never actually asked him, but there aren't five memos in between this.

So the interpretation is that it's an internal numbering system for maybe Russia stuff or maybe it's just -- I'm sorry. I don't know what the internal numbering system is, but there isn't five memos in this project between these two.

Q: So the company referenced in Company Intelligence Report, your understanding is that would be Orbis, not Fusion GPS?

A: I can't answer that. I think it's, as I said, meant to denote that it's not a government report.

Q: Were they producing -- as you noted the next apparent report 086 would be five, presumably, reports later. Were those other five reports that were being generated for Fusion GPS or --

A: No.

MR. LEVY: I don't think he said that. Go ahead.

BY THE WITNESS [SIMPSON]:

A: I mean, there aren't five reports that he did for us between these two. This is the first and second.

Q: So, again, when we look at that first one that we discussed briefly, 2016/080, it appears to be a three-page memorandum and it's dated 20 June 2016 and that shows up on the last page. Would you have received it around that time that it's dated, June 20, 2016?

A: Within a couple days, yeah. Yes.

Q: And not every single discrete memo has a date, but a number of them do. To the extent they had dates, would you have been receiving them around the time they were dated?

A: Yeah. I believe so, yes. There might be some lag, transition lag.

Q: And what was -- what use did you make of these memos?

A: These memos -- I mean, I guess I'd like to back up a little bit and explain, you know, what led to the memos, which was -- as I said, I mean, you know, we started looking at -- first we started looking at Trump's business affairs generally with some of the emphasis on associations with organized crime and in particular Russian organized crime. As the project progressed towards the end of 2015 and into 2016 we became interested in his overseas business dealings particularly because they were so opaque and seemed to involve, you know, to say the least, colorful characters.

So as we got into 2016 we were looking broadly at -- one of the things we were looking at, broadly speaking, was Donald Trump's international business dealings and, you know, through the spring of 2016, as I mentioned, we were -- you know, we looked in various places, Latin America. **He (Trump) has worked on projects all over the world, but in particular, you know, several in the former Soviet Union, Georgia, Azerbaijan, both former Soviet republics.**

So over the course of the spring I'd say -- and Russia -- we gradually began to exhaust the public record, the open source about these topics in various places. As you, you know, sort of run short on public record or open source information, you know, you need to get -- if you still want to go deeper you need to get human source.

So the purpose of this was to see if we could learn more, generally speaking, about his business dealings in Russia. What came back was something, you know, very different and obviously more alarming, which had to do with -- you know, which outlined a political conspiracy and a much broader set of issues than the ones that we basically went looking for.

You know, initially we didn't know what do with this. The main thing we did with it, the use we made of it was as intelligence, which is to understand what's happening.

So when this arrived the first indicators were starting to float around that there was something bigger going on, the government of Russia or someone was doing some hacking. I don't really remember the precise details. I just remember there were rumblings at that time about whether there had been lot of hacking and there was going to be – political digital espionage was going to be a component of the campaign.

So when this arrived it was also right around the time I think -- Trump had said weird things about the Russians and Putin and things that are very atypical for a Republican and that people found to be odd.

So when this arrived, you know, we made no immediate use of it at all in terms of, you know, giving it to anybody. **It was essentially used to inform our other researcher,** but because it was -- and because it was human source intelligence and some of it was of a personal nature, **it was not useful for the kind of things that are, you know, useful in politics, which are things that you can prove, things that you can say, things that people will believe.**

So we used it as intelligence to try and understand what was going on and, you know, obviously, as we talked about earlier, we tried to analyze this to see if it was credible. You know, I did -- you know, in the initial round of this that was the big question, was this credible.

Q: Okay. So let me stop you there for a second before we get too far because you've referred a number of times to "this" and you have a 35-page document in front of you. So I want to clarify when you said "this," in the context of answering that I assumed you were talking about the first –

A: The first memo.

Q: That's the report 2016/080? [See Above]

A: Correct.

Q: And that's the one that has the date of 20 June 2016?

A: Correct. To be totally clear, you know, **what people call the dossier is not really a dossier. It's a collection of field memoranda, of field interviews, a collection that accumulates over a period of months**. You know, they came in intermittently, there was no schedule.

You know, he'd reach a point in the reporting where he had enough to send a new memo; so he'd send one. So you won't find any real rhythm or chronological sort of system to the way they came in.

MR. MUSE: Just for clarification of "this," there are bates numbers I think that could be identified here.

MS. SAWYER: Right. So that first document, the one that we've just been talking about, has Bates Nos. 49391 to 41393. Do we need to go off the record for a moment? Let's go off the record for a moment.

Q: With regard to this document, you characterized this document as representing field interviews, I think you talked about it as human source information.

So was Mr. Steele's kind of role with regard to the project primarily conducting these types of interviews, gathering this type of what I think you referred to as human intelligence for Fusion?

A: Yes. I mean, in other cases we did other things.

MR. LEVY: Don't get into other cases.

BY THE WITNESS [SIMPSON]:

A: I can't remember specifically what I had in mind to get from him (Steele). This form of reporting was, in fact, the form that the rest of the project took, which was, you know -- I've done other kinds of research in Russia, but something this sensitive I don't think I've ever been involved in.

So in an ordinary case you would try to gather public records and you would conduct yourself in a much more open fashion.

You know, Russia is a dangerous place, it's a kleptocracy and a police state, but it's also a giant bureaucracy and in some ways it's a much more open society, much more open than the Soviet Union ever was. You can pull records for companies and that sort of thing.

Anyway, so this was unusual in what we were doing here and it's not what I had in mind when I asked him to begin collecting information on this. My expectation was of something a lot less interesting than this, more along the lines of a typical corruption investigation.

Q: You had indicated that when you received it (first memo) you found it unusual, it was sensitive information.

Did you take steps to verify any of the information?

A: We assessed it for credibility, whether it was credible. The question of the credibility of the information is obviously a big question here, can this be believed. There's other secondary questions that would follow on from that, can it somehow be used, does it have any use and that sort of thing, but the threshold question is is it credible information. You know, there were two background factors to that.

One was who is it coming from. It's coming from Chris Steele who's a guy that I've worked with for, you know, about eight or nine years and Chris, as I say, has a sterling reputation as a person who doesn't exaggerate, doesn't make things up, doesn't sell baloney. **In my business, I mean, there are a lot of people who make stuff up and sell baloney.**

So the one thing that you get good at if you do this for a while is finding reliable sources, finding reliable people who have a record of giving it to you straight and not making stuff up and not making mistakes. So from that perspective, you know, this was alarming because Chris is a credible person, he's well respected in his field, and, as I say, everyone I know who's ever dealt with him thinks he's quite good. That would include people from the U.S. government.

So the issue is where is it coming from and then the other issue is does it make sense or are there events in there that can be externally, you know, reviewed or backed up. On the question of whether it makes sense -- well, let me stay on the question of some of the events that are described. **We were aware of some of these (Trump) trips and we were obviously aware of the (Russian) hostility toward Hillary Clinton and, you know, there was a lot of general knowledge that we had that fit with this just in terms of dates and places and roles of people in the Kremlin.**

So on a surface level, you know, it was credible too, but the thing that, you know, most concerned me at this point was my own familiarity with foreign meddling in American elections, which is a subject that I've dealt with for a long time.

In the 1990s I was working at the Wall Street Journal and I wrote some of the very first stories about the Chinese government's interference in the 1996 presidential election which triggered a massive national security investigation, numerous prosecutions, lots of business for Bob Muse (Simpson's attorney of record), and a lot of congressional hearings, congressional inquiries.

And in that episode it was eventually dug out by congressional investigations that the fundraisers, the Asian fundraisers were Chinese intelligence assets. So there's ample recent historical precedent for a foreign government to interfere in American elections in a really big way and for it to be an intelligence operation.

So I knew all of that while reading this and digesting it for the first time. I also knew because I also knew because I've done a lot of reporting on Russia about the Kremlin's interest in American politics, European politics, disrupting the politics of other countries, and, in fact, one of the last things I did when I was a reporter at the Wall Street Journal was report on several stories of government investigations, FBI investigations into American politicians who had been corrupted allegedly by the Russians.

Sort of my departure point from journalism was a series of stories and conferences I attended where a lot of American and European intelligence officials were expressing great alarm at the resurfacing of Russian intelligence operations in western capitals and the new twist on it which seemed to be that these guys seemed to be getting involved in politics in ways that they hadn't previously. So I knew all that when I read this.

SIMPSON SAYS:
RUSSIANS "MAKING FRIENDS" WITH REPUBLICANS

MS. SAWYER

Q: Okay. So if I can stop you there.

It sounds like the components -- you can tell me if there were more -- that you considered in assessing the credibility of this was Mr. Steele, his background, his reputation, overall the fact that you had information and knowledge of Russia meddling in other countries' elections, and then the broader work of Russia to disrupt political systems of other countries?

A: I covered that. I also would add that the China case was for me in my journalistic career a formative event that took -- you know, consumed years of my reporting and was about, you know, a Chinese intelligence operation to swing the '96 election to the Democrats. The only other thing I'd add to all that is, again, in the mid-2000s one of the stories I wrote -- actually, I wrote a couple different stories about

a Russian oligarch having a meeting with <u>Senator John McCain</u> shortly before the 2008 presidential election

and another story or set of stories about Manafort and his involvement with some Russian and Ukrainian oligarchs who were considered to be suspicious or corrupt. So I also knew -- or I formed an opinion or impression that:

the Russians were interested in making friends with the Republicans

and that Paul Manafort, you know, there was this previous episode involving Paul Manafort, John McCain.

So all of that was in my head when this came in which, as I say, tended to support the credibility (of the Steele Dossier) — the possibility that this information was credible.

Q: <u>You mentioned a Russian oligarch who had met with Senator McCain. Who specifically was that</u>?

A: Oleg Deripaska, O-L-E-G, D-E-R-I-P-A-S-K-A. He's not able to travel to the United States because he's banned for suspicion of ties to organized crime. He's extremely close to the Kremlin, or at least he was, and is -- I broke the story of him being banned from the United States which caused him a lot of embarrassment and trouble with his business and led to him hiring a lobbyist and trying to get involved with getting a visa to the U.S.

Q: And you had also mentioned your background knowledge of Paul Manafort and his involvement with Russian oligarchs. Can you identify who those individuals were and the basis of that knowledge?

A: The issue I specifically wrote about I believe was his work for the Party of Regions and Victor Yanukovych, Y-A-N-U-K-O-V-Y-C-H, I think and that's the Pro-Russia party or was the Pro-Russia party in Ukraine, and all that work sort of grew out of work I had done about the Kremlin working with the Russian mafia to siphon money off the gas trade between Russia and Ukraine.

Q: Was that work you had done while still a reporter with the "Wall Street Journal"?

A: Yes.

Q: So any conclusions you had reached from that, would that be material that we would be able to obtain and may already have in your public reporting?

A: My articles about this are available on the Internet.

MR. LEVY: Some of them we've produced to you already because it was responsive to your request.

MS. SAWYER: Understood.

For the Forgotten Americans

Q: And there's potentially additional work product related to the work that you had done on Mr. Manafort?

A: For the "Wall Street Journal" or later?

Q: Let's start with the "Wall Street Journal"?

A: I collected lots of information on Mr. Manafort during my years at the Journal.

Q: And then we'll get into the work on Mr. Manafort more recently. So this particular memo (of the Steele Dossier) that we've been talking about, this first one doesn't specifically mention, as far as I can see, any efforts to interfere by Russia. It does talk about potential -- as it's called in here, a **dossier** of compromising material on Hillary Clinton.

Did you take any steps to verify whether that **dossier** of compromising material existed on Hillary Clinton?

A: I will answer that, but can I just back you up a little bit. I think your observation doesn't mention anything about interfering I wouldn't agree with.

Q: Okay.

A: I mean, one of the key lines here in the second paragraph says "However, he (Trump) and his inner circle have accepted a regular flow of intelligence from the Kremlin, including on his democratic and other political rivals."

So the issue with **the Trump Tower meeting**, as I understand it, is that the Trump people were eager to accept intelligence from a foreign government about their political rivals and that is, you know, I would say, a form of interference. If you're getting help from a foreign government and your help is intelligence, then the foreign government's interfering. I mean, you know, I think that also -- of course, in retrospect we now know this was pretty right on target in terms on what it says. So anyway --

Q: In reference to you think that particular sentence?

A: I mean, it clearly refers to, you know, them (Trump campaign) being interested in and willing to – it depicts them as accepting information. What we have seen to date with the disclosures this year is they were at a minimum super interested in getting information.

Q: And when you're referencing the "disclosures this year," could you just be specific about that.

A: **The Trump Tower meeting.**

Q: So with reference to the June 9th Trump Tower meeting?

A: **Yes. Yes.**

Q: Okay.

A: I will go back to your question, but, again, it (Steele Dossier) says "Source B asserted the Trump operating was both supported and directed by Putin aimed to sew discord within the U.S.," and, you know, basically -- you know, there's a number of different ways that it seems they're trying to intervene in our politics in this memo. What was your question?

Q: I appreciate that clarification. You were actually clarifying a statement I made, which I appreciate. So you had testified a little earlier that at the point in time in which you received this first memo you used it a little more as background to inform your thinking on it, but you didn't take discrete steps. Had you -- were you involved in editing this memo in any way?

A: No.

Q: Did you give Mr. Steele any specific direction on, you know, next steps?

A: Not that I can recall, no.

Q: So at this point in time was he still operating with the understanding that he was just to engage in an open-ended project?

A: Actually it wasn't really an open-ended research project -- well, it was open-ended in scope, it wasn't open-ended in time. It was take a few weeks, see if there's anything there that's interesting, notable, important, and if we think there's reason to go on we'll make that decision at that time. So it was a short-term engagement in the beginning.

Q: And to the best you can explain to us, did the client that you were working for (Perkins Coie) know that he was engaged in this particular research or what his findings were at that point in time?..Did you interfere in any way with Mr. Steele's research, tell him not to pursue any particular avenues?

A: No.

Q: To the best of your knowledge, did anyone else give him that direction, either directly or through you, and tell him not to --

A: No.

Q: If I could just finish.

A: I'm sorry.

Q: -- and tell him not to pursue any particular avenues of research?

A: No.

Q: Do you know -- if we could just move on to kind of the next memo, which begins with Bates No. 41394 and it ends with 41396. It appears to be -- it's three pages and it has a date of 26 July 2015 and it has "Company Intelligence Report 2016/086." To the best of your recollection, was this the second memo you had received from Mr. Steele?

A: To the best of my recollection, this is the second memo.

For the Forgotten Americans

CHAPTER 18

THE FBI

SIMPSON SAYS

I learned that he (Steele) was meeting with the lead FBI guy from Rome. I don't remember when he told me that.

Then afterwards he (Steele) came back (from Rome) and said, you know, I gave them (FBI) a full briefing.

Essentially what he told me was they (FBI) had other intelligence about this matter from an internal Trump campaign source...

ENTER THE FBI – 1st TIME – JULY 2016

MS. SAWYER continues...

Q: And how did you kind of use this information?

A: **Well, I think the context of external events is important here.** I believe -- it's my recollection that what prompted this memo was, in fact, the beginning of public reporting on the hack.

I think -- what is the date again? Yeah, it's 26 July.

So by this time Debbie Wasserman Schultz has been the subject of a very aggressive hacking campaign, weaponized hack, the likes of which, you know, have never really been seen. We've seen hacking in politics before, but this kind of, you know, mass theft of e-mail and then to dump it all into, you know, the public sphere was extraordinary and it was criminal.

So the question by now of whether this was Russia and whether this might have something to do with the other information that we'd received was, you know, the immediate question, **and I think this is also -- by the time this memo was written (26 July 2016) Chris had already met with the FBI about the first memo (20 June 2016).**

So he's -- if I can interpret a little bit here.

In his mind this is already a criminal matter, there's already a potential national security matter here. I mean, this is basically about a month later and there's a lot of events that occurred in between (20 June and 26 July).

You know, after the first memo, you know, Chris said he was very concerned about whether this represented a national security threat and said he wanted to -- he said he thought we were obligated to tell someone in government, in our government about this information. **He (Steele) thought from his perspective there was an issue -- a security issue about whether a presidential candidate (Trump) was being blackmailed.**

From my perspective there was a law enforcement issue about whether there was an illegal conspiracy to violate the campaign laws, and then somewhere in this time the whole issue of hacking has also surfaced. So he proposed to -- he said we should tell the FBI, it's a national security issue. I didn't originally agree or disagree, I just put it off and said I needed to think about it. Then he raised it again with me.

I don't remember the exact sequence of these events, but my recollection is that I questioned how we would do that because I don't know anyone there that I could report something like this to and be believed and I didn't really think it was necessarily appropriate for me to do that.

For the Forgotten Americans

In any event, he (Steele) said don't worry about that, I know the perfect person, I have a contact there, they'll listen to me, they know who I am, I'll take care of it.

I said okay. You know, I agreed, it's potentially a crime in progress. So, you know, if we can do that in the most appropriate way, I said it was okay for him to do that.

Q: Okay. So let me just stop you there and let's just make sure we get the sequencing accurate.

A: Sure.

Q: So after Mr. Steele had found out the information that he put in the first of these memos, dated June 20, 2016, he approached you about taking this information to specifically the FBI, the Federal Bureau of Investigation?

A: That's my recollection.

Q: So to the best of your recollection, that request or idea came directly from Mr. Steele, not anyone else?

A: That's right.

Q: And who was involved in discussions about whether it was appropriate to take either the memo or the information in the memo to the FBI?

A: It was Chris and me. I mean, that's the only ones I remember, the two of us. The only ones I know of.

Q: You said you had asked for some time to think it over. What in particular did he articulate to you was of significant national security concern to indicate that it should be taken to the FBI?

A: His (Steele's) concern, which is something that counterintelligence people deal with a lot, is whether or not there was blackmail going on, whether a political candidate (Trump) was being blackmailed or had been compromised.

And the whole problem of compromise of western businessmen and politicians by the Russians is an essential part of -- it's like disinformation, it's something they worry about a lot and deal with a lot and are trained to respond to. So, you know, a trained intelligence officer can spot disinformation that you or I might not recognize, certainly that was Chris's skill, and he honed in on this issue of blackmail as being a significant national security issue. Chris is the professional and I'm not.

So I didn't agree with that -- it wasn't that I disagreed with it. It was that I didn't feel qualified to be the arbitrar of whether this is a national security expert. He's the pro and I'm the ex-journalist.

Q: In that regard when you say he's a professional and you're not, I take that to mean that he was the intelligence expert?

A: He was -- yes, he was the national security guy. I know a lot about politics, I know a good bit about financial crime, but, you know, my specialty was journalism and his was security.

Q: And with specific regard to the issue of blackmail, what were the FACTS that he (Steele) had gathered that made him concerned about the possibility of blackmail and who did he think was going to be blackmailed?

A: Well, the facts are beyond what's here I don't have any additional facts. The alleged incident that's described here is the one that he was referring to. As I say, I don't have really any additional information beyond this except that -- I mean, it's probably in here somewhere actually, but it's **well known in intelligence circles that the Russians have cameras in all the luxury hotel rooms** and there are memoirs written about this by former Russian intelligence agents I could quote. So the problem of "kompromat" and "kompromating" is just endemic to east-west intelligence work. So that's what I'm referring to. That's what he's referring to.

Q: Got it. So that would be in the summary (of memo 2: above) the kind of third dash point down where it mentions --

A: Yes, that's right.

Q: -- that FSB -- what is your understanding of who or what FSB is?

A: It's a successor to the KGB. I mean, nominally it's the domestic intelligence agency on the domestic side of what was the KGB. In practice it's sort of the preeminent intelligence organ of the Russian state, government.

Q: And do you recall when you and Mr. Steele decided that he could or should take this to the FBI approximately the time frame of that?

A: I believe it was sometime around the turn of the month. It would have been in late June or at latest early July. That's my recollection.

Q: And Mr. Steele was the one who was then responsible for doing the initial outreach to them and making that contact?

A: Yes. Well, I mean, let's be clear, this was not considered by me to be part of the work that we were doing. This was -- to me this was like, you know, you're driving to work and you see something happen and you call 911, right.

It wasn't part of the -- it wasn't like we were trying to figure out who should do it. He (Steele) said he was professionally obligated to do it (go to FBI). Like if you're a lawyer and, you know, you find out about a crime, in a lot of countries you must report that. So it was like that. So I just said if that's your obligation, then you should fulfill your obligation

Q: And were you a part of those conversations with -- that Mr. Steele had with whoever his contact was at the FBI?

A: No.

For the Forgotten Americans

Q: Do you have any knowledge of when that first (Steel-FBI) conversation actually then took place?

A: Over the last several months that this has become a public controversy I've learned the general date and I believe it was if first week of July, but I don't believe he told me if he told me the time, I don't remember when he told me.

Q: And that information about that time, that first week of July, where does that come from?

A: It comes from news accounts of these events and conversations between Chris and I and some of my -- presumably my business partners too.

Generally speaking, we have, as you know, not been eager to discuss any of this in public and there's been a lot of speculation and guessing and stories, many of which are wrong. So when an incorrect story comes out we would, you know, talk about it. So, you know, in the course of those kinds of things I generally obtained a sense of when things occurred that I might otherwise not be able to provide.

Q: And do you know who it is that Mr. Steele contacted and talked with at the FBI?

A: I did not know at the time. I believe I know now, but I don't have authoritative information on that. I didn't -- yeah. I didn't know who it was in July.

Q: And do you now know who that was?

A: I think I know, but Chris never told me. I figured it out eventually based on other sources and other information, but that was not until December or November.

Q: December of -- November or December 2016?

A: November, December 2016. It was after the election.

Q: And what is your understanding from what you've been able to put together of who that would have been?

A: My understanding of?

Q: Of who Mr. Steele would have talked to at the FBI.

A: I believe it was official named [REDACTED].

Q: And we had talked about that discussion that you had with Mr. Steele about potentially going to the FBI. You had indicated it was just two of you having those conversations and coming to that decision.

Once the decision was made, did you share that decision with anyone, that he was going to go to the FBI with this information?

A: I think we're not able to answer that.

MR. LEVY: He's going to decline to answer that question.

BY MS. SAWYER:

Q: Did you seek anyone else's approval for him to go to the FBI?

A: No.

Q: Did anyone ever encourage you to ask him on to go to the FBI?

A: No.

Q: Did anyone discourage you from having him go to the FBI?

A: No.

Q: Do you know whether Mr. Steele when he had that first meeting, which you said occurred in the first week of July, do you know whether Mr. Steele actually gave the FBI this document that we've been talking about, the intelligence report 2016/080?

A: I don't know.

Q: With regard to providing -- what was the goal -- as you understood it, what was the purpose of the kind of goal in taking this to the FBI from Mr. Steele's perspective?

A: I mean, for him it was professional obligations. I mean, for both of us it was citizenship. You know, people report crimes all the time.

Q: So beyond reporting -- certainly if I'm mischaracterizing please let me know, but beyond reporting what he believed was an issue of national security and a potential crime, I think you had said kind of a potential crime in progress, do you know whether he requested that the FBI open an investigation?

A: I don't know that. I mean, all he told me in the immediate aftermath was that he filled him in. I can talk generally about the FBI and what happens when you give them information because I know that from years of experience, but generally, you know, you don't ask them to do it. There's no ask.

Q: But you don't know what concrete steps they (FBI) may have taken once they got the information from him (Steele)?

A: I do not. Of course we know now that shortly thereafter they (FBI) got a vice award on one of the people who's dealt with in here. He's not dealt with in this memo, but he's dealt with in the later memos. I don't know there's any connection between these events. I do know in Director Comey's testimony he said -- I'm sorry. Maybe I'm skipping ahead. As far as I know, they didn't – I don't know what they did.

Q: So then with regard to Mr. Steele's ongoing work, I presume that his work then continued after you got this first memo?

A: Yes.

Q: Was there a discussion about whether and when he would take information to the FBI?

A: Not that I recall. After the initial memo he told me that he had briefed him. I don't remember anything specific about the issue arising again other than to say generally that as the summer progressed the situation with the hacking of the Democrats and the efforts by the Russians to influence the election and the possibility that the Trump organization was, in fact, doing things to curry favor with the Russians became more and more serious as external developments occurred.

So, for instance, they changed the Republican platform, which is addressed in here. Carter Page shows up in Moscow and gives a speech. He's a campaign advisor and he gives a speech about dropping sanctions.

Trump continues to say mysterious things about what a great guy Putin is. So I vaguely recall that these external events prompted us to say I wonder what the FBI did, whoops, haven't heard from them.

<u>So that was basically the state of things through September (2016).</u>

SIMPSON SAYS:
<u>STEELE MET FBI –AGAIN - IN ROME</u>

Q: So do you know whether or not Mr. Steele did have any subsequent conversations with the FBI after that initial conversation in the first week of July 2016?

A: Yes, I do. He did.

Q: So can you explain the next incident where you know that Mr. Steele met with the FBI?

A: Yes. I guess what I'd like to explain is what I knew at the time and what I know now. It was September (2016) and obviously the controversy was really front and center now in the election.

I can't remember whether the intelligence community had come out with their statement, but, you know, there was a lot of concern in Washington and in the U.S. about whether there was a Kremlin operation to interfere with our election and there was a lot of debate throughout this period about whether they were trying to help Trump or just trying to cause trouble.

But there wasn't much debate that they were up to something.

So, you know, I'm dealing with Chris on the underlying reporting and by this time my concern, you know, was -- I was very concerned because Chris had delivered a lot of information and by this time we had, you know, stood up a good bit of it. Various things he had written about in his memos corresponded quite closely with other events and I began, you know, to view his reporting in this case as, you know, really serious and really credible.

So anyway, we were working on all of that and then he (Steele) said, hey, I heard back from the FBI and they want me to come talk to them and they said they want everything I have, to which I said okay.

He said he had to go to Rome, I said okay. He went to Rome.

Then afterwards he (Steele) came back (from Rome) and said, you know, I gave them (FBI) a full briefing. I'll add because I didn't consider this to be -- you know, there was no objective here politically because you can't -- in an ordinary election.

I know from my decades of dealing with U.S. elections that you can't expect the government or the FBI to be of any use in a campaign because the DOJ has rules against law enforcement getting involved in investigations in the middle of a campaign and this was obviously -- you know, this obviously became a huge issue. Anyway, because it wasn't really part of the project in my mind I didn't really ask a lot of questions about these meetings. I didn't ask who he met with, I didn't ask, you know, much of anything, but he did tell me that he gave –

Q: Before we get to that, which I do want to hear, I just want to get a sense of the chronology.

A: Sure.

Q: -- you had said the FBI then came back and contacted Mr. Steele?

A: That's my understanding.

Q: <u>When did that, to the best of your knowledge, take place?</u>

A: Mid to late September.

Q: So in that intervening time period Mr. Steele continues his research, he also continues to provide you with memos?

A: Yes.

Q: And at no point in that time between July -- the first week of July when he first met with the FBI and then mid to late September did you suggest to him that he should go back to the FBI?

A: Not that I recall. What I believe I may have said was have you heard anything from the FBI because by then it was obvious there was a crime in progress. So I just was curious whether he'd heard back.

Q: And when you say it was obvious that there was a crime in progress, what specifically are you referencing?

A: ESPIONAGE. They were hacking into the computers of Democrats and think tanks. That's a computer crime.

Q: So the thing that was apparent was Russia or somebody had engaged in cyber-intrusion and computer crimes?

A: Yes.

For the Forgotten Americans

Q: So do you know whether or not Mr. Steele was directed -- you said you did not direct him or ask him to go back to the FBI -- whether anyone else either directly or indirectly asked him to go to the FBI after his July 5th --

A: To my knowledge, no one else told him to report this. He may have conferred with his business associates, but I don't know.

Q: And you said that meeting with the FBI, you said Mr. Steele said he had to go to Rome for this meeting. Do you otherwise know who he met with?

A: This gets into the chronology of what I learned when. At some point I learned that he (Steele) was meeting with the lead FBI guy from Rome. I don't remember when he told me that.

Q: And did you have a name associated with who that was?

A: Not at that time.

SIMPSON SAYS:
FBI SOURCE IS A TRUMP INSIDER

Q: You said that he told you of the meeting with the FBI in Rome in mid or late September, that he "gave them a full briefing"?

A: A debrief, I think, is what he probably said. They (FBI) had debriefed him (Steele). I don't remember him articulating the specifics of that. You know, my understanding was that they would have gotten into who his sources were, how he knew certain things, and, you know, other details based on their own intelligence.

Essentially what he told me was they had other intelligence about this matter from an internal Trump campaign source
and that – that they -- my understanding was that they believed. Chris at this point -- that they (FBI) believed Chris's information might be credible because they had other intelligence that indicated the same thing and one of those pieces of **intelligence was a human source from inside the Trump organization.**

Q: Did you have any understanding then or now as to who that human intelligence source from inside the Trump campaign might have been?

MR. LEVY: He's going to decline to answer that question.

MS. SAWYER: On what basis?

MR. LEVY: Security.

BY THE WITNESS [SIMPSON]:

A: We had been really careful -- I was really careful throughout this process to not ask a lot of specific sourcing questions. There are some things I know that I just don't feel comfortable sharing because obviously it's been in the news a lot lately that people who get in the way of the Russians tend to get hurt.

MR. LEVY: And I would just add that there are privileges and obligations that might be implicated in the disclosure of any source.

BY MS. SAWYER:

Q: Was this individual (Trump Insider FBI Informant) also a person who had been a source for Mr. Steele, without identifying who that was?

A: No.

Q: So this was someone independent of Mr. Steele's sources who potentially had information also on the same topics?

A: Yes. I mean, I don't think this implicates any of the issues to say I think it (Trump insider and FBI source) was a voluntary source, someone who was concerned about the same concerns we had.

MR. DAVIS: I'm having a hard time hearing you.   Please speak up.

BY THE WITNESS [SIMPSON]:

A: It was someone like us who decided to pick up the phone and report something.

Q: And your understanding of this, does that (Trump insider and FBI source) come from Mr. Steele or from a different source?

A: That comes from Chris, yes.

Q: And when did he (Steele) share that (source) information with you?

A: I don't remember exactly.

Q: Do you think it was around the same time that he had met with the FBI, so mid to late September of 2016?

A: I think more likely early October.

Q: Do you know whether when Mr. Steele met with the FBI he provided them with the memos that he would have had at that point in time, which would have been mid to late September of 2016?

A: I don't know that. He didn't tell me that. He did say they (FBI) asked him for -- they wanted to know everything he had, but whether that would include getting paper I don't know.

Q: And did he indicate that he had cooperated fully and given them whatever information he had available?

A: Yes. In the course of these, you know, discussions, you know, he indicated to me this (FBI person) was someone he had worked with previously who knew him and that they (Steele and FBI person) had a -- they worked together.

Q: By that (FBI) person you're referring to in Rome?

A: Yes.

Q: Just to finish up on the interactions with FBI, do you know were there any additional interactions between Mr. Steele and the FBI?

A: There was some sort of interaction, I think it was probably telephonic that occurred after Director Comey sent his letter to Congress (28 OCTOBER 2016) reopening the investigation into Hillary Clinton's e-mails.

SIMPSON SAYS:
HE AND STEELE ANGRY AT FBI

Simpson continues: On That episode, you know, obviously created some concern that the FBI was intervening in a political campaign in contravention of long-standing Justice Department regulation.

So it made a lot of people, including us, concerned about what the heck was going on at the FBI.

So, we began getting questions from the press about, you know, whether they were also investigating Trump and, you know, we encouraged them to ask the FBI that question. You know, I think -- I'm not sure we've covered this fully, but, you know, we just encouraged them to ask the FBI that question.

On October 31st "The New York Times" posted a story saying that the FBI is investigating Trump and found no connections to Russia and, you know, it was a real Halloween special.

===

"Investigating Donald Trump, F.B.I. Sees No Clear Link to Russia"

By Eric Lichtblau and Steven Lee Meyers Oct. 31, 2016

WASHINGTON — For much of the summer, the F.B.I. pursued a widening investigation into a Russian role in the American presidential campaign. Agents scrutinized advisers close to Donald J. Trump, looked for financial connections with Russian financial figures, searched for those involved in hacking the computers of Democrats, and even chased a lead — which they ultimately came to doubt — about a possible secret channel of email communication from the Trump Organization to a Russian bank.

Law enforcement officials say that none of the investigations so far have found any conclusive or direct link between Mr. Trump and the Russian government. And even the hacking into Democratic emails, F.B.I. and intelligence officials now believe, was aimed at disrupting the presidential election rather than electing Mr. Trump...(See article at:

www.nytimes.com/2016/11/01/us/politics/fbi-russia-election-donald-trump.html)

===

Simpson continues:

Sometime thereafter the FBI -- I understand Chris severed his relationship with the FBI out of concern that he didn't know what was happening inside the FBI and there was a concern that the FBI was being manipulated for political ends by the Trump people and that we didn't really understand what was going on. **So he stopped dealing with them.**

Q: I do want to get to the timing on that. I know that I'm getting close to the end of my hour. Can I just ask you a general question on the memos that we were talking about? I had asked you specifically about the first one, if you had in any way -- first of all, with regard to the packet (Steele Dossier) on whole,

did you have any input or involvement in the drafting of these or input for the research?

A: No.

Q: And did you edit any of them in any way?

A: No.

Q: So these were documents (memos comprising Steele Dossier) that you were just receiving from Mr. Steele?

A: Yes. I mean, the only qualifier I'd add is I'm sure I said things like Paul Manafort was just named campaign manager, what do you know about him, that kind of thing.

Q: I do want to get into some more specifics about kind of what steps and what items you may also clarify, but I do want to make sure, if I could have your indulgence, just that we -- well, we can finish up the FBI part on our next hour because it sounds like there's a little more to finishing that. So our hour is up. If you'll just give me a moment.

Okay. So we'll go ahead and go off the record.

It is 2:58. (A short break was had.)

MR. DAVIS: We'll go back on the record. It's now 3:09.

EXAMINATION BY MR. DAVIS:

Q: Mr. Simpson, do you know Emin Agalarov?

[NOTE: Questions on Prevezon – not in Steele Dossier omitted]

Q: You previously mentioned that Fusion had hired subcontractors beyond Mr. Steele to work on the Trump project. Was there any overlap of other subcontractors between the Trump investigation and the Prevezon work?

A: Not to my recollection.

Q: And had Fusion worked with Mr. Steele prior to this project regarding Mr. Trump?

A: Yes.

Q: And had you previously paid him or Orbis?

A: I believe so, yeah.

Q: And had Fusion been paid by him or Orbis as well?

A: Yes, I believe so.

Q: And are you aware of any interactions Mr. Steele had with the FBI prior to his work on the investigation of Mr. Trump and his associates?

MR. MUSE: Could you repeat that?

MR. DAVIS: Are you aware of any interactions with Mr. Steele with the FBI prior to his work on the investigation of Mr. Trump and his association?

BY THE WITNESS [SIMPSON]:

A: I was not at the time, but I am now.

Q: Did you have reason to believe that in his (Steele's) prior position within British intelligence he would have interacted with the FBI?

A: Yes, he's told me that.

Q: Do you believe that the FBI generally considers sources more credible if they have previously provided reliable information?

A: That's my understanding.

Q: Was Mr. Steele's reportedly successful history in working with the FBI a factor in deciding to hire Orbis for the Trump project?

A: No.

Q: Do you know **Christopher Burrows**?

A: Yes.

Q: Do you know if he worked on the Trump- Russia project with Orbis?

A: I do not.

Q: Do you know **Sir Andrew Wood**?

A: No.

Q: Are you aware he's an associate of Orbis Business Intelligence?

A: I am aware of that as of now. I didn't know it -- I don't know when I learned of it, but I didn't know it last year, much of last year.

Q: Did Fusion ask Orbis (Steele's company) to undertake other actions beyond preparing the memoranda containing the allegations regarding Mr. Trump and his associates?

A: Not that I specifically -- I'm sorry. In connection with that engagement?

Q: In connection with that engagement.

A: Not that I specifically recall.

Q: Did you communicate with Mr. Steele other than through these memos? Did you have phone calls and e-mails with him?

A: Mostly we spoke by phone.

MR. FOSTER [Jason Foster, Chief Investigative Counsel, Chairman Grassley]: You did also e-mail with him?

MR. SIMPSON: Nothing -- I don't believe I had anything substantive. E-mail security is a major problem. So, generally speaking, we would try to communicate telephonically on an encrypted line.

MR. FOSTER: Did you have another method of communicating with him via text.

MR. SIMPSON: I mean, we used encrypted methods of communicating. Part of the security concern we have involve there's been a lot of attempts to break into our systems. So I prefer not to get into a lot of that, but suffice to say we use secured encrypted systems.

MR. FOSTER: Regardless of the details of how you did, do you retain copies of written communications that you may have engaged with him through some other secure method?

MR. SIMPSON: Generally not.

MR. FOSTER: You have not retained?

MR. SIMPSON: Generally we use things that can't be stolen because they no longer exist.

MR. FOSTER: Disappearing messages, auto deleting messages?

MR. SIMPSON: That sort of thing, yes, that's correct.

MR. FOSTER: I just needed a verbal answer.

MR. SIMPSON: Yeah. Sorry.

BY MR. DAVIS:

Q: You previously mentioned the relationship with Mr. Steele was more collaborative than a manager-employee and I think you referenced mentioning as an example Paul Manafort's been named campaign chairman, what do you know about him. Did you collaborate with Mr. Steele on the content of the memos even if he did the drafting?

A: No, generally speaking. I was managing a much bigger project and he's a reliable provider. So I did very little tasking.

Q: You mentioned other subcontractors were focusing on other regions in which the Trump organization has business. Were those other subcontractors retained until the election or how long did their engagements last?

A: It was ad hoc.

For the Forgotten Americans

CHAPTER 19

THE MEDIA, MCCAIN & U.K.

SIMPSON SAYS

we were encouraging the media to ask questions about whether the FBI was, in fact, investigating these matters.

I where the issue of this (Steele Dossier) research was discussed and the essence of it, I guess, was conveyed to Senator McCain and to David Kramer from Andrew Wood.

and that Senator McCain had followed up on it as to what more there was to know about these allegations, this information.

that he (Steele) broke off, which implies that he told him he didn't want to have anything more to do with them (FBI).

I had spoken with reporters over the course of the summer and through the fall about the investigations by the government...

SIMPSON'S CREDIBILITY IS CHALLENGED

BY MR. DAVIS:

Q: One point I'd like to clarify from Ms. Sawyer's questioning. I believe you said that Mr. Steele had told you that the FBI had a source from inside the Trump organization and I believe she referred to a source from inside the Trump campaign. Do you know which is the accurate --

MR. LEVY: He's not going to get into the details of that source.

MR. DAVIS: I'm not asking for any particular details. It was characterized differently by you and by counsel. I just wanted to make sure.

BY THE WITNESS [SIMPSON]:

A: I don't know.

MR. FOSTER: So you don't know whether it was the organization or the campaign, in other words?

MR. SIMPSON: That's correct.

MR. FOSTER: Meaning the business versus the campaign.

BY MR. DAVIS:

Q: And did Mr. Steele tell you that the FBI had relayed this information to him?

A: He didn't specifically say that.

Q: I'm going to have you take a look at one of the filings --

MR. FOSTER: I thought you said earlier that he did say the FBI told him.

MR. SIMPSON: I think I was saying we did not have the detailed conversations where he (Steele) would debrief me on his discussions with the FBI. He would say very generic things like I saw them, they asked me a lot of questions, sounds like they have another source or they have another source.　　He wouldn't put words in their mouth.

BY MR. DAVIS:

Q: I'm going to have you take a look at one of the filings by Mr. Steele's attorneys in the lawsuit against him and Orbis in the United Kingdom. This will be Exhibit 4. (Exhibit 4 was marked for identification.)

LONDON - STEELE IS DEFENDANT SUIT V. RUSSIAN

If you could please turn to page 2 and read paragraph No. 8. That states

At all material times Fusion was subject to an obligation not to disclose to third parties confidential intelligence material provided to it by the Defendants in the course of that working relationship without the agreement of the Defendants."

<u>Is that a correct description of your understanding of how the material was to be treated?</u>

MR. MUSE: There's also a context to that who the Defendants are in other such matters.

MR. DAVIS: Sure. The Defendants are Orbis Business Intelligence Limited and Christopher Steele.

BY THE WITNESS [SIMPSON]:

A: What's the question?

Q: Is that an accurate description of what you understood the obligations to be with that material (the Steele Dossier)?

A: I mean, that's hard for me to answer. There's a mutual expectation of confidentiality, and if that's what you read that as saying, then yes, there's a mutual expectation of confidentiality.

Q: Was that expectation established by contract?

MR. LEVY: We're not going to talk about contracts with clients.

BY MR. DAVIS:

Q: Was it established by practice?

A: I guess I'll just reiterate we do confidential work together and we treat all matters as confidential. He's pretty good at sticking to that and so am I.

Q: Was any of the information included in the memoranda Orbis prepared during the Trump investigation not considered "confidential intelligence" under this understanding such that Fusion was not required to obtain Orbis's permission in order to disclose it?

A: I don't really understand the question.

Q: I'm saying if the understanding is that you weren't to disclose confidential intelligence material, were the memos (Steele Dossier) confidential intelligence material, the dossier memos?

A: They're confidential, yes.

MR. MUSE: Hold on one second. Here's the mischief that's created by that. Someone else is sending this and you're asking what they mean. There may be direct answers to those questions if you ask direct questions, but to do it in the frame of reference of someone else putting forth a piece of evidence, which this is, it inevitably creates confusion.

The reference to the document adds nothing to his knowledge. It's just simply a point of reference by you, but it doesn't add anything to what he might be saying. So I think the better way to get at it is simply to ask direct questions.

MR. DAVIS: There are two parties to this, at least, and we've got one's description. I'd like to know if he agrees with that description.

MR. MUSE: But even within what do they mean by this is the question. I mean, what do they mean by this sort of paragraph. You're asking him for an interpretation. He can answer questions about the relationship.

MR. DAVIS: I'm asking him to give an interpretation of their agreement in terms of what he did.

MR. MUSE: And therein lies the problem.

MR. DAVIS: But if it's an agreement to which he's a party, there's a basis for that understanding.

MR. MUSE: I don't think that's the way the rule works.

MR. FOSTER: Well, I think the bigger mischief from my point of view is the fact that we're trying to get an understanding of what the contractual relationship was. You're telling us you're not going to provide us with details about that contractual relationship, you're not going to provide us with copies of any nondisclosure agreements, contracts we've asked for and we don't have. So we're asking him for his understanding of what obligations he had.

MR. LEVY: And that's outside the scope of this interview. Go ahead.

MS. SAWYER: Can I in general ask that you guys all speak up a little bit because we're right under the blower.

MR. LEVY: Will do.

MR. FOSTER: The record will reflect we are not raising our voices. To be clear, you're instructing him not to answer that question because you think it's outside the scope of what he agreed to come here to talk about voluntarily?

MR. LEVY: That's not what I said. You had made a comment about contracts, and I just wanted to make sure that obviously the Chair and the Ranking Member have agreed those questions are not part of the scope of this interview. That said, I've now forgotten what the pending question was. So if Patrick wants to restate it he can and we can evaluate it.

ENTER: THE MAINSTREAM MEDIA

MR. DAVIS: Sure. In general we're asking questions about distribution of the material within the (Steele) **dossier** which was the scope of the agreement. If you look at page 4 of that same exhibit, paragraph 30, Steele's attorneys state:

"The Defendants" -- and again, that's Orbis Business Intelligence and Christopher Steele –

"*did not however provide any of the pre-election memoranda to any of the media or journalists, nor did they authorize anyone to do so, nor did they provide the confidential December memorandum to media organizations or journalists, nor did they authorize anyone to do so.*"

To the best of your knowledge, did Orbis ever authorize Fusion to make any disclosures of the memoranda to the media?

MR. LEVY: Just before we get into this question, this paragraph began with a sentence you did not read and it says "In the first sentence of subparagraph 8.2.5 as noted." I don't know what they're referring to. Maybe you do. Can you show us that?

MR. DAVIS: I don't have that with me at the moment, but I'll see if we can find it. Regardless, did Orbis ever authorize you to share the memoranda with the media?

BY THE WITNESS [SIMPSON]:

A: **I'm not sure I can answer this in -- I'm not sure I know the answer to this.**

MR. LEVY: If you don't know, then...

MR. SIMPSON: It's a little confusing.

MR. FOSTER: You don't know whether or not Orbis or Mr. Steele authorized you to distribute the memos to the media?

MR. SIMPSON: I think what I would like to say is that we had discussions about, you know, information as opposed to memos and, you know, at various times in talking to reporters about the Trump-Russia connection, you know, things – those discussions would be informed by what's in the memos.

MR. FOSTER: So are you saying that you may have provided information from the memos to the media without discussing whether or not – without getting permission specifically from Steele or Orbis?

MR. SIMPSON: What I'm saying is we discussed that. No. I'm saying we discussed generally the wisdom of answering questions from reporters about different matters, what we could say and what we couldn't say.

MR. FOSTER: And in those discussions did he ever authorize you to discuss the information contained in the memoranda with the media?

MR. SIMPSON: **As I've stated before, this is not a master-servant relationship.** We worked together. Sometimes he's working for my clients, sometimes I'm working for his. So we might jointly make a decision, but it's not a sort of can I do this, yes you can do that kind of relationship. So if they -- so I hope that's responsive.

MR. FOSTER: So did you ever share either the memos or the content of the memos with the media independently of him without having discussed it with him?

MR. SIMPSON: **I think what I said was I had spoken with reporters over the course of the summer and through the fall about the investigations by the government** and the controversy over connections between -- alleged connections between the Trump campaign and the Russians. Some of what we discussed was informed by Chris's reporting. So whether that was -- I don't think there's any sense that that was an unauthorized thing to do.

MR. DAVIS: On page 5 --

MR. FOSTER: Is it something that you discussed with him that you were doing?

MR. SIMPSON: We would discuss inquiries that we had received from reporters, yes.

MR. FOSTER: And that you were answering?

MR. SIMPSON: To the best of our ability. I mean, we obviously didn't tell people about the existence of these things for a long time.

BY MR. DAVIS:

Q: On page 5 of that same exhibit, paragraph 32 there's a portion of the sentence -- and I'll just read this for background before we move on to another segment. I think this is relevant for context. There's a portion here in which Steele's attorneys state that he gave -- that the Defendants gave:

"Off-the-record briefings to a small number of journalists about the pre-election memoranda in late summer/autumn 2016."

I'd like to provide Exhibit 5 which is the second filing by Mr. Steele's attorneys.

MS. SAWYER: Patrick, you've represented this one as the second filing. Are we sure these are --

MR. DAVIS: Second for the purpose of this interview, second one we're referencing.

MS. SAWYER: Were these documents that were requested or obtained from a third party in the course of the investigation?

MR. DAVIS: These were documents that were published in the media. I believe the second one was published by "McClatchy".

MS. SAWYER: And what about the first?

MR. DAVIS: That was the one published by "The Washington Times".

(Exhibit 5 was marked for identification.)

===

EXHIBIT 5: "The Washington Times" -

"Ex-spy admits anti-Trump dossier unverified, blames Buzzfeed for publishing"

By Rowan Scarborough – "The Washington Times" - April 25, 2017

Christopher Steele, the former British spy who wrote the infamous anti-Donald Trump dossier, acknowledges that a sensational charge his sources made about a tech company CEO and Democratic Party hacking is unverified.

In a court filing, Mr. Steele also says his accusations against the president and his aides about a supposed Russian hacking conspiracy were never supposed to be made public, much less posted in full on a website for the world to see on Jan. 10.

He defends himself by saying he was betrayed by his client (FUSION GPS) and that he followed proper internal channels by giving the dossier to Sen. John McCain to alert the U.S. government...

In his final December dossier memo — his 16th — Mr. Steele accused Mr. Gubarev and his web-hosting companies of hacking the Democratic Party computer networks with pornography and bugging devices. Mr. Gubarev calls the charge fiction and filed a lawsuit in February.

Mr. Steele's court filing portrays him as a victim of Fusion GPS — the firm that hired him with money from a Hillary Clinton backer...

The final Steele memo, after accusing Mr. Gubarev then recounts from previous memos a **supposed trip Mr. Cohen took to Prague** in late August to meet with Russian agents and devise a plan to cover up the purported Trump team's role in the hacking...

Mr. Cohen calls the dossier "fabricated." He has shown that he was in California at the time and has never been to Prague. He told "The Washington Times" that he has instructed his attorneys to investigate a lawsuit against Mr. Steele

The fact that Mr. Steele acknowledges that he put unverified "raw intelligence" into his December memo casts further doubt on his research techniques for the entire 35-page dossier.

SECOND ONE: "McClatchy" -

"John McCain faces questions in Trump-Russia dossier case"

BY KEVIN G. HALL on July 11, 2017 5:00 AM

WASHINGTON – Sen. John McCain faces questions in a defamation lawsuit about leaks leading to publication of the now-infamous dossier that alleged Donald Trump's campaign had connections to Russian operatives, McClatchy has learned.

The dossier compiled by former British spy Christopher Steele and his London firm, Orbis Business Intelligence Ltd., amounted to a collection of uncorroborated reports of collusion gathered as political research for sale to Trump's opponents. It proved explosive when published by online news site BuzzFeed on Jan. 10.

Now, two lawsuits — one in the United States and a second in the U.K. — are being brought by lawyers for Aleksej Gubarev, a Cyprus-based

Internet entrepreneur whom Steele's Russian sources accused of cyber spying against the Democratic Party leadership.

According to a new court document in the British lawsuit, counsel for defendants Steele and Orbis repeatedly point to McCain, R-Ariz., a vocal Trump critic, and a former State Department official as two in a handful of people known to have had copies of the full document before it circulated among journalists and was published by BuzzFeed...

==

MR. DAVIS continues...

Q: So with the second one on page 8 of Exhibit 5, under the response to 18 Steele's attorneys state:

The journalists initially briefed at the end of September 2016 by the second Defendant and Fusion at Fusion's instruction were from "The New York Times", "The Washington Post", "Yahoo News", "The New Yorker", and "CNN".

The second Defendant -- that would be Mr. Steele –

subsequently participated in further meetings at Fusion's instruction with Fusion and "The New York Times", "The Washington Post", "Yahoo News", which took place in mid-October 2016. In each of those cases the briefing was conducted verbally in person.

"In addition, and again at Fusion's instruction, in late October 2016 the second Defendant briefed the journalist from "Mother Jones" by Skype. **No copies of the pre-election memoranda were ever shown or provided to any journalist by or with the authorization of the Defendants (STEELE and ORBIS).**

The briefings involved the disclosure of limited intelligence regarding indications of Russian interference in the U.S. election process and the possible coordination of members of Trump's campaign team and Russian government officials.

To the best of your knowledge, is that a full and accurate account of all the news organizations with which Fusion and Mr. Steele shared information from the memoranda.

A: I'd say it's largely right.

Q: Are there any that have been omitted?

A: Yeah. I think there's at least one thing misidentified. There might have been another. I can't specifically think of it, but I think this is incomplete, that maybe one of the broadcast networks is misidentified. I just don't have a tally of this. It's mostly right.

Q: By broadcast network I assume you mean CNN is incorrect,?

For the Forgotten Americans

A: I think so.

Q: Do you recall which network it was?

A: I think it was ABC.

Q: Did you attend these meetings with Mr. Steele?

A: Yeah. Yes.

Q: Did any other Fusion associates attend?

A: Possibly, yes.

Q: Can you identify them?

Q: Do you recall the specific dates of these meetings?

A: No.

Q: I believe the filing says end of September 2016. Does that comport with your recollection?

A: Yes.

Q: Was this, as far as you know, before or after Mr. Steele had had his second meeting with the FBI?

A: I don't remember. Sorry.

Q: Did Mr. Steele ever indicate to you whether the FBI had asked him not to speak with the media?

A: I remember Chris saying at some point that they were upset with media coverage of some of the issues that he had discussed with him.

Q: Sorry. I didn't hear.

A: He never said they told him he couldn't talk to them (media).

Q: Do you recall which journalists you spoke to at each of these organizations and what information from the memoranda was revealed?

A: I remember some of them and I remember some of the names, yeah, some of the people I talked to and some of these discussions.

Q: Can you tell us what those were?

MR. LEVY: The answer to that question goes to confidential conversations that's been declined to answer.

MR. FOSTER: Sorry. Confidential what?

MR. LEVY: The answer to that question might implicate privilege …and he's not going to answer the question.

MR. FOSTER: What's the privilege?

MR. LEVY: First amendment, confidentiality.

MR. FOSTER: Confidentiality agreement, contractual obligation, is that what you're talking about?

MR. LEVY: No. Just talking to confidential sources, First Amendment issue. We can discuss it later after the interview.

BY MR. DAVIS:

Q: Mr. Steele's filing indicates that these meetings occurred at Fusion's instruction. Is that correct, did you initiate these meetings and instruct Mr. Steele to participate in them?

A: I'd just reiterate the nature of our relationship was that -- I might propose something and he might agree to do it, but it was not a -not a military style relationship where I gave the orders and he carried them out.

Q: Was part of the purpose of your investigation to share information with journalists?

A: I think that's a fair statement. To the extent -- I mean, I'm sorry. Could you be clear. You mean the project overall?

Q: Yes, investigating Mr. Trump and his associates.

A: As I said earlier, in any project, and that would include this one, the objective is to gather relevant information, and some of that **information was gathered for other purposes and some of it was gathered for the possibility that it might be useful to the press.**

Q: Did your client instruct you to have these meetings?

MR. LEVY: The answer to that question might implicate privilege...

BY MR. DAVIS:

Q: Do you have any reason to believe that Mr. Steele passed any information on to journalists without Fusion?

A: Without me -- you mean without me participating, without me authorizing it? Can you be more specific?

Q: Sure. Let's start without you participating. The filing references meetings that both you and Fusion jointly had with journalists. Do you believe he (Steele) had any meetings with journalists without you present?

MR. LEVY: Without Mr. Simpson physically present?

MR. DAVIS: For physical meetings or via Skype, without him aware of them contemporaneously.

A: That's a difficult question to answer because I don't know what I don't know, but I don't have any reason to believe that he did anything that I didn't authorize or approve.

Q: Jason may have already touched on this, but did Fusion disclose hard copies of the memoranda to any journalists?

MR. LEVY: The answer to that question might implicate privilege or obligations. HE has said that neither Mr. Simpson nor Fusion GPS provided the dossier to BuzzFeed, he's going to decline to answer your question respectfully.

THE U.K. AND SENATOR MCCAIN

BY MR. DAVIS:

Q: Still with Exhibit 5 on page 2, the responses to 4 and 6. Here the attorneys for Orbis and Mr. Steele --

MR. LEVY: Where are you again?

BY MR. DAVIS:

Q: Page 2, the response to 4 and to 6. Here the attorneys for Orbis and Mr. Steele state:

The duty not to disclose intelligence to third parties without the prior agreement of the Defendants" -- again, that's Orbis and Mr. Steele -- *"do not extend to disclosure by Fusion to its clients, although the Defendants understand that copies of the memoranda were not disclosed by Fusion.*

A: Where are you You're on page 2 -- okay. I see it now.

Q: -- "do not extend to disclosure by Fusion to its clients, although the Defendants understand that copies of the memoranda were not disclosed by Fusion to its clients." Further down on that same page in response to a question about whether Fusion's clients, insofar as disclosure to them, was permitted, could themselves disclose the intelligence from Orbis, the filing responds: *Defendants understood that the arrangement between Fusion and its clients was that intelligence would not be disclosed.*

Is that a correct statement of the relationship between you and the client, did Fusion not disclose the memoranda or information contained therein to its clients?

MR. LEVY: He's not going to get into discussion with the client because of privileges … implicated by the answer to that question.

BY MR. DAVIS:

Q: Do you believe this filing is accurate in those paragraphs?

MR. LEVY: Again, to comment on that he would have to talk about client communications that are privileged and might implicate privilege.

BY MR. DAVIS:

Q: Mr. Simpson, do you believe that any confidentiality obligations regarding the memos did not extend to law enforcement and intelligence services?

A: Yes. I mean, I -- well, in general I think that in the course of any sort of confidential business lawyers or other professionals engage in if they come across information about a possible terrorist attack or a mafia operation they should report it, yes, and that that is, in fact, not covered by ordinary confidentiality.

WAS STEELE PAID BY FBI?

BY MR. DAVIS:

Q: Was Fusion aware of the reports that the FBI considered -- let me rephrase. Was Fusion aware that the FBI considered paying Mr. Steele to investigate Mr. Trump and his associates?

A: When?

Q: At any time.

MR. LEVY: When you say "paying," what do you mean by that?

MR. DAVIS: Providing money.

MR. LEVY: For a fee? Are you talking about reimbursements?

MR. DAVIS: Fees or reimbursements in this context.

BY THE WITNESS [SIMPSON]:

A: We've learned that. We know that now. In fact, it was --

MR. LEVY: Learned what?

BY THE WITNESS [SIMPSON]:

A: Well, we learned -- sometime after the election we learned that **Chris had discussed working for the FBI on these matters after the election and that that didn't happen.**

Q: Did Mr. Steele discuss that (FBI payment) with you at the time?

A: He didn't discuss it -- I don't remember exactly when he mentioned this to me, but he mentioned to me at some point I think after the election that he (Steele) had discussed this with them.

MR. FOSTER: So prior to news reports to that effect? In other words, you learned it from him not from the news; is that right?

MR. LEVY: Wait. You asked two different questions. I'm trying to figure out which one you want him to answer.

MR. FOSTER: The last one.

MR. LEVY: What was the last one?

MR. FOSTER: You learned it from the news and not from him? Are you saying you learned it from him?

MR. LEVY: Learned what from him?

MR. FOSTER: That he discussed with the FBI having the FBI pay Mr. Steele.

MR. SIMPSON: I don't remember.

MR. LEVY: The witness is yawning. Let's take a break.

MR. MUSE: We will attribute that to fatigue as opposed to the questions.

MR. FOSTER: Let's go off the record. It is 3:55. (A short break was had.)

For the Forgotten Americans

THE FBI-STEELE-FUSION-MCCAIN-U.K:

MR. DAVIS: We'll go back on the record. It's now 4:05..

Q: Mr. Simpson, did anyone from Fusion ever communicate with the FBI regarding information in the memoranda or other allegations regarding Mr. Trump and his associates?

A: From Fusion, did anyone from Fusion communicate with the FBI? No, no one from Fusion ever spoke with the FBI, to the best of my knowledge.

Q: Did you ever exchange any e-mails with them?

A: We did not communicate with them by e-mail either.

Q: Do you know any current or former FBI personnel?

MR. LEVY: As a general matter?

MR. DAVIS: Yeah, as a general matter.

BY THE WITNESS [SIMPSON]:

A: As a general matter I'm sure I do. I know current and former law enforcement officials. I go to a lot of crime conferences and things like that.

Q: Were any of them consulted as part of this investigation?

A: Not to my recollection.

[**NOTE:** No mention of Associate Deputy Attorney Bruce]

Q: Was the amount of Fusion's compensation in the Trump investigation dependent on the FBI initiating an investigation of Mr. Trump or his associates?

A: No.

Q: Was the amount of Orbis's compensation dependent on the FBI initiating an investigation of Mr. Trump and his associates?

A: No.

Q: Other than Senator McCain, who we'll discuss later, did Fusion or Orbis disclose any of the memoranda information contained therein or related information from Mr. Steele with any elected officials or staff in Congress?

A: I don't recall having done so, no.

Q: If we could turn briefly back to Exhibits 4 and 5. I just want to reference two things.

MR. LEVY: I also want to clarify in the premise of that question there were factual assertions made that may or may not be true to which the witness did not respond.

MR. DAVIS: Sure. Understood. To be clear, we obviously were not referencing any disclosures to this committee as part of the committee's inquiry.

<u>SENATOR MCCAIN AND THE DOSSIER</u>

MR. DAVIS continued:

Q: So on Exhibit 4, page 3, paragraph 21A, Mr. Steele's attorneys state that the post-election **dossier** memoranda was provided to a senior United Kingdom government national security official acting in his official capacity.   In Exhibit 5 on page 2 -- I'm sorry -- page 5, the response to similarly references disclosing that memoranda to the UK national security official.

<u>Mr. Simpson, to the best of your knowledge, were the memoranda or information contained therein disclosed to foreign governments?</u>

A: I have no knowledge of this beyond what you're showing me. I can tell you about, you know, what I know about Chris's encounter with David Kramer and how all that came about.

If Chris specifically said something to me about showing this to one of his government officials I don't remember it. So...

MR. LEVY: Why don't you walk them through.

BY THE WITNESS [SIMPSON]:

A: If you want to know the rest of the story, I'm happy to walk you through it.

Q: Sure, we can do that.

A: So after the election obviously we were as surprised as everyone else (that Trump had won) and Chris and I were mutually concerned about whether the United States had just elected someone who was compromised by a hostile foreign power, more in my case whether the election had been tainted by an intervention by the Russian intelligence services, and we were, you know, unsure what to do.

Initially we didn't do anything other than to discuss our concerns, but we were gravely concerned.

At some point a few weeks after the election Chris called me and said that he had received an inquiry from David Kramer, who was a long-time advisor to Senator McCain, and that according to -- Kramer told Chris that he had run into Sir Andrew Wood at a security conference in Halifax, Nova Scotia and that Kramer was accompanying Senator McCain to this conference and that the three of them had had an unscheduled or unplanned encounter

> **where the issue of this (Steele Dossier) research was discussed and the essence of it, I guess, was conveyed to Senator McCain and to David Kramer from Andrew Wood.**

I don't remember whether Andrew Wood's name was specifically given to me by Christopher Steele at that time. It was later given to me. It later became an accepted fact that Chris had mentioned him to me. I believe he probably mentioned it.

For the Forgotten Americans

[NOTE: Wikipedia States: **Sir Andrew Marley Wood** *is a former British diplomat...* **In 1964,** *he was posted to Moscow by the British Diplomatic Service. Following a range of diplomatic posts he served as British Ambassador to Yugoslavia from 1985 to 1989. From* **1995 to 2000 Wood served as British Ambassador to Russia and Moldova before** *retiring from diplomatic service*].

But anyway, he (Steele) did say someone that he worked with in the past who was a former UK government official with experience in Russia had had this conversation with David Kramer and John McCain

and that Senator McCain had followed up on it as to what more there was to know about these allegations, this information.

So Chris asked me do you know David Kramer, and I said yes, I've known David Kramer for a long time. David Kramer is part of a small group of people that I'm sort of loosely affiliated with. We've all worked on Russia and are very concerned about kleptocracy and human rights and the police state that Russia has become, in particular the efforts of the Russians to corrupt and mess with our political system.

So we shared this concern going back to when I was at the "Wall Street Journal" and that's how I met David. He was working at the State Department as assistant secretary for human rights, and I was reporting on human rights and corruption in Russia. So I told Chris he's legit.

David is someone I've known for a long time and he knows a lot about these issues and he's very concerned about Putin and the Kremlin and the rise of the new Russia and criminality and kleptocracy.

So he said, well, can we trust him? And I said yes, I think we can trust him. He says he wants information to give to Senator McCain so that Senator McCain can ask questions about it at the FBI, with the leadership of the FBI.

That was essentially -- all we sort of wanted was for the government to do its job and we were concerned about whether the information that we provided previously had ever, you know, risen to the leadership level of the FBI. We simply just didn't know.

It was our belief that Director Comey if he was aware -- if he was made aware of this information would treat it seriously.

Again, at this time, you know, while we believed that we had very credible reporting here, you know, what we really -- we just wanted people in official positions to ascertain whether it was accurate or not. You know, we just felt that was our obligation.

So I said to Chris I think we can trust him, and he said okay. Well, he was here (U.K), I met with him, and I told him what happened. Now he's back in Washington and, you know, I'm going to hand him to you.

I don't remember whether I called David or David called me, I just don't remember, but we got in touch and he, you know, asked me -- we met.

Q: And after you met how did he -- did you provide the memoranda to

MR. LEVY: Sorry. Finish your question.

BY MR. DAVIS:

Q: -- did you provide the memoranda to him?

MR. LEVY: The answer to that question might implicate privilege and other obligations. So he's going to decline to answer the question.

BY MR. DAVIS:

Q: Did Mr. Steele represent to you that Orbis or Mr. Wood had initiated this contact with Mr. Kramer and Mr. McCain to share the **dossier** information?

A: Well, that has two parts on that question. I think I can answer the first part which I think answers the second.

Anyway, he did not describe this as having been initiated by Orbis. He described this as a chance encounter at a security conference where, you know, someone who had some knowledge of these matters shared it with Senator McCain and David Kramer and that caused David Kramer to follow up with Chris and that it was passive.

In other words, it was initiated by Mr. Kramer.

Q: Did Mr. Steele describe anyone else being involved at the Halifax international security conference in this discussion?

A: Not that I can recall.

Q: According to the official attendee list for that conference, Mr. Akhmetshin was also there. To the best of your knowledge, was he involved in any capacity in the effort to discuss the **dossier** information with Mr. Kramer and Mr. McCain?

A: That's the first time I've received that information. So I don't have any knowledge.

Q: And you haven't spoken with Mr. Akhmetshin about that, I assume?

A: No.

Q: In addition to the disclosures we have already discussed, to whom did Fusion GPS provide the memoranda, information contained therein, or related information from Orbis?

MR. LEVY: Beyond what you've discussed?

MR. DAVIS: Anyone we've left out.

MR. LEVY: The answer to that might implicate privilege or other obligations. So he's going to decline to answer the question.

BY MR. DAVIS:

Q: To the extent there's any portion of the answer to that question that would not implicate those privileges, I would ask that you reveal those.

A: I'm not sure I see how I could answer that question without getting into privileged areas.

MR. FOSTER: Again, what privilege?

MR. LEVY: We can discuss it at the end. It's a voluntary interview. He's declining to answer that.

BY MR. DAVIS:

Q: Did any Fusion employees communicate with any foreign governments or foreign intelligence agencies about the memoranda or the information contained therein?

A: I don't believe so, certainly not knowingly.

Q: Did you and Mr. Steele ever discuss any communications he had with foreign government officials about the information in the memoranda?

A: It would be difficult -- nothing specific that I recall. There are parts of the memos that talk about information that foreign government officials provided in the course of their research, but beyond what's in the memos I don't really have any recollection.

Q: Do you know who paid for Mr. Steele's trip to Rome to meet with the FBI?

A: I have read recently that -- I think in a letter from Senator Grassley that the FBI reimbursed the expense, but to be clear, I mean, that's it. **He (Steele) was, to my knowledge, not been compensated for that work or any other work during this time.**

MR. FOSTER: I'm sorry. You're saying that Fusion did not pay for the trip?

MR. LEVY: Go ahead and answer the question.

MR. SIMPSON: I don't think we did. I have no information that we paid for it.

Again, this sort of emphasizes, you know, the point I was making earlier which was this was something that I considered to be something that Chris took on his own based on his professional obligations and not something that was part of my project. So it makes sense to me that he was reimbursed by them (FBI) not us.

BY MR. DAVIS:

Q: To clarify, you were saying his interactions with the FBI were not part of your project?

A: They obviously grew out of the project, but as he explained it to me, you know, when you learn things in your daily life that raise national security considerations you're obligated to report them.

So that wouldn't have anything to do with my client's goals or project.

Q: But in your briefings with journalists you did reference his interactions -- Mr. Steele's interactions with the FBI, correct?

A: At some point that occurred, but I don't believe it occurred until very late in the process.

Q: Can you estimate when in the process?

A: It was probably the last few days before the election or immediately thereafter.

Q: So the meetings in September that you referenced, you didn't reveal Mr. Steele passing on information to the FBI?

MR. LEVY: Can you repeat the question. Sorry.

MR. DAVIS: So in your meetings with journalists in September you didn't reference Mr. Steele's interactions with the FBI or passing on of information to them?

BY THE WITNESS [SIMPSON]:

A: I don't recall.

MR. DAVIS: I think my hour is up.

MR. FOSTER: Off the record at 4:21.

(A short break was had.)

MORE ON STEELE-FBI RELATIONSHIP REVEALED

MS. SAWYER: We'll go back on the record.   It's 4:30.

EXAMINATION BY MS. SAWYER:

Q: I wanted to return to our conversation about interactions that Mr. Steele had with the FBI. We had been talking about a second time he met in Rome. Besides that meeting and the first meeting in early July, are you aware of any other meetings or conversations that Mr. Steele had with the FBI?

A: I think I was just recounting that he vaguely said that he (Steele) had broken off with them (FBI) over this concern that we didn't really know what was going on. I'm sorry to be vague, but we just didn't understand what was going on and he said he had broken off with them.

Q: When you say "we" did not understand what was going on, who are you referring to as the "we"?

A: Chris and I, mostly just the two of us. There was a lot of public controversy over the conduct of the FBI. I remember discussing it with many people, but this conversation was between the two of us.

Q: And what was the time frame of when Steele said he had broken off with the FBI?

A: I can -- I don't know exactly, but it would have been between October 31st and election day.

MS. QUINT [Lara Quint, Chief Counsel for Rhode Island Democrat Senator Whitehouse]:

Q: October 31st was when you said there was an article --

MR. SIMPSON: In "The New York Times". There was an article in the "New York Times" on October 31st that created concern about what was going on at the FBI.

> **[NOTE:** See above NYT article: **"Investigating Donald Trump, F.B.I. Sees No Clear Link to Russia"** (Page 108)**]**

MS. QUINT: Because it wasn't consistent with your understanding of the investigation?

MR. SIMPSON: Exactly.

BY MS. SAWYER:

Q: And I think, just to be clear, this was an article you had talked about that both revealed that Director Comey had alerted Congress to something about the Clinton e-mail investigation?

A: No. That happened a few days previous. I don't know the exact date that he sent the letter to Congress, but this was an article specifically about -- it was disclosing the existence of an FBI investigation of Trump's ties to Russia, which, to my recollection, was the first time that anyone reported that the FBI was looking at whether the Trump campaign had ties to the Kremlin.

But at the same time saying that they had investigated this and not found anything, which threw cold water on the whole question through the election.

Q: And was that -- just to tie it together when you were talking previously, was that in connection with your conversation with journalists where you directed them to ask the FBI as to whether there was an investigation going on?

A: I'm not going to get into specific news organizations or reporters or stories, but I would restate that this was during the period when

> **we were encouraging the media to ask questions about whether the FBI was, in fact, investigating these matters.**

I'll add that, you know, a lot of what we were talking to the media about were things in the public record, specifically Carter Page, Paul Manafort had resigned over allegations of illicit relationships with Russian oligarchs and Ukrainian oligarchs.

So there was, you know, a lot of open source public information pointing towards the possibility that the Russians had infiltrated the Trump campaign. So we spoke broadly to reporters and encouraged them to look into this.

Q: And did you ever come to find out who the journalists had spoken with at the FBI about the existence of an investigation into Russian interference and possible ties to the Trump campaign?

A: No.

Q: So you had indicated that Mr. Steele said he had -- I think your phrase was "broken off" with the FBI. What did you understand that to mean?

A: That Chris was confused and somewhat disturbed and didn't think he understood the landscape and I think both of us felt like things were happening that we didn't understand and that we must not know everything about, and therefore, you know, in a situation like that the smart thing to do is stand down.

Q: And had he been reaching out affirmatively to the FBI and providing them with information or were they reaching out to him and he was simply responding to their requests?

A: The first contact was initiated by Chris to someone that he said he knew.

Q: And now you're just going back to the July contact?

A: Yes. The September briefing or debriefing in Rome I believe I understood -- to this day I understand that to have been initiated by the FBI. Subsequent contacts during this period I just don't know.

Q: Do you know if there were any contacts after that second meeting in Rome between then and the point in time which occurred sometime between October 31st and the election day when he stopped communicating with the FBI, do you know if there actually were any conversations or meetings between Mr. Steele and the FBI?

A: He didn't literally tell me about specific contacts. I just recall that there was

> **that he (Steele) broke off, which implies that he told him he didn't want to have anything more to do with them (FBI).**

I believe he also mentioned that they didn't like media coverage, that there was media coverage of, you know, FBI interest in Donald Trump. I don't know what it was that they didn't like.

Q: And I think you've already answered this question, but to the best of your knowledge,

> did Mr. Steele ever obtain payment from the FBI for actual research that he was doing on Russian interference or on possible ties between the Trump campaign and Russia?

A: He told me he did not, and I have no independent information other than what he told me. I don't believe he ever received compensation for working on anything related to Trump and Russia.

For the Forgotten Americans

CHAPTER 20

MORE ON DOSSIER & CARTER PAGE

SIMPSON SAYS

Generally speaking, most of this information is useful for making decisions and trying to understand what's going on, but it's not -- doesn't have much use beyond that unless you can independently verify it.

Most of this I did not seek to independently verify and was relatively new information.

In British intelligence the methodology's a little different from American intelligence. There's a practice of being faithful to what people are saying.

Basically because everyone in Russia, you know, more or less works for the government

There's all this money flowing in the United States from Russia, it probably flows in under some sort of diplomatic status

I read a lot of books and studies on Russia and organized crime.

MS. SAWYER continues:

Q: I'm going to direct your attention back to what we marked as Exhibit 3 (Steel Dossier), which is the series of memos that you had received from Mr. Steele in the course of his work.

We talked about the first memo and we also talked about the second memo to some degree.

You were explaining to me why you believed the second memo (Co. Intelligence Report 2016/86), which starts at page 41394 (page in the Senate Exam material), came about, why he had generated that report or done that research, and you had indicated that there was much more public reporting on the hacking. I think you had mentioned -- that's when you mentioned Debbie Wasserman Schultz.

So with regard to that memo, were there any particular things that you independently verified?

A: I just need to review it here for a second.

Q: Sure. (Reviewing document.)

A: Most of this (memo two 2016/86) I did not seek to independently verify and was relatively new information.

I was aware at the time of connections between Russian intelligence and cyber criminals, and I was aware at the time that the Russian mafia and Russian cyber crime was a subcontractor to the Russian intelligence services. So this comported with my general knowledge of these matters, but a lot of the specifics was new information to me.

The only things in here that I specifically recognize from other work or from other research was that the -- the allegation that the telegram encrypted messaging system, which is an app, had been compromised by Russian intelligence and that someone else in the business of cyber security had told me that too who was in a position to know.

I don't remember who that was, but I was told that by an American.

And issues of Russian criminal operations with names like Booktrap and Maddel rings a bell to me or did ring a bell to me at the time. There's been a great deal – there had been a great deal at this time even of U.S. law enforcement activity against organized Russian cyber crime.

Q: This memo which is dated 26 July – it actually bears the date 2015.

A: I noticed that.

Q: Is that just, as far as you understand it, a typo or mistake? Was it actually 2016?

A: Yes.

Q: Then similarly with what I have -- and I'm just doing it in the order that it was Bates-stamped and appeared on BuzzFeed -- there's a two-page report and it bears the Bates Nos. 41397 and 41398 and it has a company report number 2016/095. This one has the title "Russia/U.S. Presidential Election, Further Indications of Extensive Conspiracy Between Trump's Campaign Team and the Kremlin."

Q: Did you do any independent verification of these facts (memo)?

A: I did some work on aspects of this. We were separately -- you know, my team and myself were separately investigating various things in here.

So I can't talk about this as a verification, but I was analyzing this.

MR. FOSTER: Speak up, please.

BY THE WITNESS [SIMPSON]:

A: I analyzed this information in the same manner I analyzed the other stuff.

Q: So based on the work that you were doing did any of that independent work that you did alter the content of this?

A: No.

Q: So it was in addition to whatever was provided in this memo, this two-page memo?

A: Yes, that's right.

Q: And to the best that you can recall, can you tell us what you were learning at the same time about the topics covered in this memo?

A: Yes. Could I just clarify something? I assume this is exactly how it was published and someone mixed up the sequence of the memos.

So the next memo's numbered 94 and is dated July 19th and this one is 95 and is not dated, I don't believe. Maybe that's why they got mixed up. But in any event, what I would loosely call the Carter Page memo (see below insert) came before this conspiracy memo.

So with that caveat I can say we were investigating just based on open sources and, you know, other methods, more public information Carter Page's trip to Russia.

We watched tapes of it, we did background work on Carter Page, I did research on his business dealings, and in the course of trying to analyze -- you know, **this is some new detail here about how the operation is working in the Kremlin and how they are trying to use influence and it comports with my knowledge and Chris's knowledge of how the Kremlin does this, which is they offer people business deals as a way to compromise them.**

And, in fact, you know, to my knowledge, this is a much bigger issue than personal indiscretions when it comes to the way the Kremlin operates and is something I know a fair bit about.

So we looked into Carter Page and we also looked into Igor Sechin and whether Sergei Ivanov was in a position to be managing the election operation, which is what 94 talks about, and we determined that he was. I, you know, independently verified he does have a deputy who's very obscure named Igor Divyekin It's spelled two different ways here.

I believe the correct spelling is D-I-V-Y-E-K-I-N.

BY MR. MUSE [one of Simpson's attorneys]:

Q: Can you give the Bates number of the document you're looking at.

MR. SIMPSON: This one is 41399.

BY MS. SAWYER:

Q: And just for the record, it's a two-page document, 41399 to 41400, and it has the date, I think you indicated before, 19 July 2016.

Is this the memo (memo four 2016/094) that you said you referred to as the Carter Page memo?

A: Yes.

Q: And you were explaining that in the sequencing this one came before the document that actually in terms of Bates numbers --

A: Right.

Q: -- comes before it which we had talked about which had the company report No. 095. So 94 came to you before 095 -- report No. 095; is that correct?

A: That's my recollection.

Q: So with regard to the research you were also doing, is it also just true that whatever independent research you were doing did not then get incorporated into document company report 2016/94, the Carter Page memo?

A: That's correct. We essentially segregated this reporting from other things we were doing for reasons we discussed earlier.

A lot of this is human intelligence, it's not the kind of thing that you would share with almost anyone basically. A lot of the work that we do is public record research.

Generally speaking, most of this information is useful for making decisions and trying to understand what's going on, but it's not -- doesn't have much use beyond that unless you can independently verify it.

So our reports are full of footnotes and appendices and court records and that sort of thing.

Q: So is it fair to characterize the research that you were doing as kind of a separate track of research on the same topic sometimes?

A: I think so. I wouldn't say it was completely separate because, for instance, on some subjects I knew more than Chris. So when it comes to Paul Manafort, he's a long-time U.S. political figure about whom I know a lot.

But his (Steele's) reporting -- you know, so there may have been some bleed between things I told him about someone like Manafort, but most of these characters neither of us know much about and it's really just he's faithfully reporting information to him that's being reported to him by his network. **In British intelligence the methodology's a little different from American intelligence. There's a practice of being faithful to what people are saying.**

So these are relatively straightforward recitations of things that people have said. Obviously as we talked about before, you know, disinformation is an issue that Chris wrestles with, has wrestled with his entire life. So if he believed any of this was disinformation, he would have told us.

Q: And did he ever tell you that information in any of these memos, that he had concerns that any of it was disinformation?

A: No.

What he said was disinformation is an issue in my profession, that is a central concern and that we are trained to spot disinformation, and if I believed this was disinformation or I had concerns about that I would tell you that and I'm not telling you that.

I'm telling you that I don't believe this is disinformation.

Q: And then on the memo, the Carter Page memo, which is company report 2016/94, you said that you had done -- you, Fusion -- you, Glenn Simpson had done some research into Carter Page, including Mr. Page's business dealings?

A: Yes.

Q: Is that information that you still have?

A: I don't know. I haven't looked for it. I don't know.

Q: You also specifically mentioned Igor Sechin and maybe work that you had done research into Sechin. Is that work that you would also still have?

A: I don't know if I have anything specific on Sechin. Sechin is a well-known character. I collect, you know, research on various people who are oligarchs or mafia figures. I don't think I have any specific reports on Sechin, but I know a lot about him. He's, you know, sort of Putin's No. 1 compadre in the kleptocracy.

Q: And with regard to Carter Page, did you reach any findings, conclusions about his business dealings, about him, about his connections in particular to, you know, Russia?

A: Yes.

Q: And can you share what those were?

A: Carter Page seemed to us to be a typical person who the Russians would attempt to co-opt or compromise or manipulate. He was on the younger side, a little bit -- considered to be a striver who was ambitious and not terribly savvy, and those are the kind of people that the Russians tend to compromise. That was the general sense we had.

He was also, you know, from early on described as somewhat eccentric.

There was a -- I remember quite clearly there was a bit of a -- when we were talking to reporters about him because he was all over the news for this trip to Russia and we had done -- there was a fair amount of open source on his consulting firm, his complaint that he'd lost money on Russian investments and he owned stock in Gazprom.

And he was really mad about the sanctions and he went over there in this hastily-arranged trip to speak to this school and that was all pretty unusual, but there's a lot of skepticism in the press about whether he could be linked between the Kremlin and the Trump campaign because **he (Carter Page) seemed like a zero, a lightweight.** I remember being able to kind of explain to people that's exactly why he would end up as someone who they would try to co-opt. Of course, you know, when we talk about things in the **dossier** that are confirmed, this is one of the things that I think really stands out as notable, which is that **Chris identified Carter Page as someone who had -- seemed to be in the middle of the campaign, between the Trump campaign and the Kremlin, and he later turned out to be an espionage suspect who was, in fact, someone that the FBI had been investigating for years.**

Q: So beyond what is in the **dossier**, did you kind of find any evidence that he had actually been compromised? I'm speaking of Carter Page.

A: Well, the definition of compromised is someone who has been influenced sometimes without even their knowledge. We had reason to believe that he had, in fact, been offered business deals that were -- that would tend to influence him, business arrangements.

Q: And do you have the records of those (Page) business deals that you had collected?

A: Yeah. I don't think so. Most of that was, in fact, reporting that we did with other people who knew him from the business world.

===

CARTER PAGE GOES ON THE RECORD

On 05 FEB 2017 - Carter Page gave a rare interview on "The Ingraham Angle" (Fox News Channel) and said the following:

> *I gave a speech (in Russia) and there was one senior government official who spoke after me. He was walking out of the building after he gave his speech and we had a very brief conversation for less than 10 seconds. It was really an exchange of pleasantries...*
>
> **I've never met him (Igor SECHIN) in my entire life.**

And in response to Russia offering Carter Page 19% of an oil company, he responded to host Laura Ingraham:

> **You know what's interesting about that is, if you do the math on that, 19% had a market value of $11 billion dollars.**

And in response Ingraham's question about the FBI, he said:

> *I sent a letter to (FBI) Director Comey on Sunday, September 25th, 2016; two days after the defamatory articles came out against me...I told him that everything was totally false. If you have any questions about this "witch hunt", which is what I called it, please don't hesitate to call me.*
>
> *I would love to set the record straight with your agents.*
>
> *I told him that I've been in contact with the Intelligence Community for many, many years and I'd be happy to help out, you know, again in providing you (Comey) some accurate insight.*

==

MS. SAWYER continued:

Q: And then just the next memo that we had touched on, 2016/95, it has Bates numbers 41397 to 398, it does not bear a date on it.

Do you recall roughly when you received this particular report?

A: Sometime in midsummer.

Q: The next report, which is 2016/097 which is two pages, has the date of 30 July 2016. Just by the numbers it would appear to maybe have come between those two.

Does it seem logical that it came sometime between July 19th and July 30th?

A: That seems logical.

Q: And then just in general, with regard to this particular memo did you do any research to verify this information that was in this memo?

MR. LEVY: Beyond what he said as a general matter?

MR. MUSE: I'm sorry. You were going back and forth. Which one in particular?

MS. SAWYER: This is memo No. -- it has Company Intelligence Report 2016/095, it's Bates 19 numbers 41397 and 41398.

MR. MUSE: Thank you.

BY MS. SAWYER:

Q: Was there particular information in this memo that you did verify?

A: One of the things I did, which is pretty typical of how I would sort of analyze things, was I looked at the Russian pension system to determine if, in fact, the Russian government was distributing lots of pension payments to Russian immigrants in the United States, and I found some reports from the Social Security Administration and other places describing this system.

Basically because everyone in Russia, you know, more or less works for the government, there's a lot of −

there's a large number of Russian emigres in the United States who receive pension payments that are paid through the embassies and various people, Russian lawyers and others who we became interested in in the course of this investigation seem to be involved in that process.

I'm not saying they did anything illegal. I'm just saying, you know, we looked at this system, and as someone who does a lot of money laundering work this was an interesting thing that I hadn't heard about.

There's all this money flowing in the United States from Russia, it probably flows in under some sort of diplomatic status.

So if there's sanctions on Russia and the Russians can't move money in the United States for most things, this would, in fact, be an ideal mechanism for moving money into the United States for whatever purpose, for some kind of illicit purpose. I think that's a pretty good example of the kind of general work I would do to determine whether there's some base level of credibility to the things we're getting.

Q: And in answering that you said that some of the officials that you had identified as involved in this effort seemed to come up with regard to the pension disbursements. Who specifically are you referring to?

A: We identified a lawyer in Sunny Isles Beach, Florida who said she previously worked for Gazprom and just had on her professional Website or someplace that she was -- she had some kind of relationship with the Russian embassy in dealing with these pension issues.

Q: And do you recall that lawyer's name?

A: I don't.

Q: Anyone else besides that individual?

A: If I could look at this for a second.

Q: Sure. (Reviewing document.) **BY THE WITNESS [SIMPSON]:**

A: I don't have a clear recollection of this. I'm sorry. I thought there was another name in here that we had looked at, but I don't see it in this memo.

Q: To the extent you have records about this and the individual in Sunny Isles, would you at least look for them and let us know whether you would be willing to provide them to the committee?

MR. LEVY: Counsel has the request.

BY MS. SAWYER:

Q: Just moving on to the next memo, which is Company Intelligence Report 2016/097, it bears the Bates Nos. 401 and 41402, it's a two-page memo dated 30 July 2016.

Again, when you take a look at that, was there anything that you independently verified that comes out of this memo?

(Reviewing document.)

BY THE WITNESS [SIMPSON]:

Q: Okay. Then Company Intelligence Report 2016/100, was there any information there that you either independently verified or had independent research on any of the individuals mentioned in there. It mentions Sergei Ivanov, Dmitry Peskov.

MR. MUSE: If I may, some clarification. When you say is there anything that you independently verified that comes out of the memo, are you talking -- it's a little confusing because the memo comes in, he already knows some information, but I think he's generally said that he's not doing a draft of the memo beforehand and yet your question seems to permit that possibility.

MS. SAWYER: No. I appreciate the clarification.

Q: Just to be clear, I'm not trying to -- what we're trying to determine is is there information that either you had in your possession that corroborated and verified this (memo six) or even went beyond what was in this and amplified information on any of these individuals relevant to Russia's interference or possible ties with the Trump campaign?

A: Yes. I'm trying to be as helpful as I can. The thing that we worked on with regard to Sergei Ivanov, who was the head of what's called the head of administration which we confirmed from open sources is kind of an internal Kremlin intelligence operation, and that Ivanov according to experts on Russia, the Russian military, Russian intelligence, does, in fact, run this internal Kremlin intelligence operation that sort of sits atop the FSB and the SVR, the GRU, which are the other agencies specifically tasked with areas of intelligence, military for the GRU, foreign for the SVR, domestic for the FSB.

Before I got this memo I didn't know about this internal Kremlin structure. It was either this one or the previous one. So in the course of saying who is this Ivanov guy, you know, we looked at Ivanov and found journal articles and other public information about his long history of intelligence. He's a veteran of the FSB, his long history with Vladimir Putin, and his role atop this internal operation.

In particular I remember reading a paper by a superb academic expert whose name is Mark Galeotti, G-A-L-E-O-T-T-I, who's done a lot of work on the Kremlin's black operations and written quite widely on the subject and is very learned. So that would have given me comfort that whoever Chris is talking to they know what they're talking about.

Q: With regard to that just in general, I did want to ask you not to identify based on the particular sources, but

Did Mr. Steele ever share with you who his sources were?

MR. LEVY: That conversation, if it occurred would implicate obligations and he's going to decline to answer that question.

MS. SAWYER: And is that based just on the -- can you just articulate the obligations so we can understand them.

MR. LEVY: It's a very sensitive security issue and I just don't -- in a transcript where there's no assurance of confidentiality it's not a discussion we want to have here.

BY MS. SAWYER:

Q: And do you know whether he shared his sources with the FBI?

A: I don't. I don't know.

MR. FOSTER: What was the answer?

MR. SIMPSON: Sorry. I don't know whether he shared his sourcing with the FBI.

MS. SAWYER: Can we just take a minute. We can go off the record.

Just with sensitivity toward the lateness of the day and in the interest of time it would just be helpful -- and I'll give you as much time as you need to take a few minutes and, if you could, look through the remaining memos and let us know if anything kind of stood out to you, if there were things that either did not ring true at the time and that you were concerned about or things in particular that in addition to what's in here you had independent research about you could share with the committee in the context of our investigation. Is that a clear request?

MR. MUSE: Heather, may I make a suggestion?

MS. SAWYER: Sure.

MR. MUSE: Why don't we break for a few minutes so he can look at it....

MS. SAWYER: I understand where you're going. So yeah.

MS. SAWYER: Why don't we take a five-minute break and I'll ask whatever remaining questions we have on the **dossier**.

MR. FOSTER: We'll go off the record at 5:11. [a short break was had]

MS. SAWYER: We're back on the record at 5:20.

Q: We appreciate you are walking through some of these and we understand your general practice and I want to make sure I'm characterizing this accurately.

When you would get the memos you would -- from Mr. Steele you would review them, you would see if they resonated with information that you already knew and other research you may already have done.

I think you already told me that you don't recall at the time anything jumping out at you as patently inaccurate; is that fair to say?

A: Yes, that's fair to say.

Q: And I had just asked you to review and I appreciate you taking the time to review the additional memos which would just run from Bates No. 41405 to 41425 to just try to determine for the committee if research that you had been doing on the separate track on some of these topics in particular amplified the work in the **dossier**.

MR. LEVY: You say "amplified the work in the **dossier**," what do you mean?

MS. SAWYER: Both kind of verified and maybe gave you some additional information and insights on either the factual allegations in them or whether or not the key players identified had also engaged in either similar or related behavior on Russian -- you know, related to Russian interference.

A: I'd say that's generally right. **I read a lot of books and studies on Russia and organized crime.** So over the years I just have a lot of residual knowledge of some of the people and subjects that are covered in the memos.

Q: Okay. So nothing certainly jumped out at you and then as --

A: Nothing jumped out at me --

Q: -- as inconsistent with information gained from other sources?

A: That's correct.

Q: And did you have any reason to believe either then or now that Mr. Steele would have kind of fabricated any of the information that he included in any of these memos?

A: No.

Q: I do want to return to a few of the topics and a few of the specifics, but I think I'll hold that until the next round because I have a few other just follow-up questions for you. It had come up in the last round that there was a meeting and some information was provided to Mr. Kramer. Were you still -- at the time that occurred were you, Fusion GPS, still working on behalf of a client who had engaged you to do research as part of the presidential election campaign or did that occur after that engagement ended?

A: It occurred after the engagement had ended.

Q: And besides Mr. Steele, did you discuss sharing information with Mr. Kramer with anyone else?

A: Not that I recall.

Q: My colleagues had also asked you about meetings and particularly that occurred between June 8th and June 10th of 2016 and some of the individuals involved in those meetings. As a general matter, did you discuss the work you were doing related to the presidential election campaign with -- did you ever discuss that with Natalia Veselnitskaya?

A: I don't believe I ever discussed it with her. I'd just add that she doesn't speak much English. So the possibilities are almost none. I didn't discuss it with her.

Q: Do you have any reason to believe that she knew that you were doing work – opposition research work on then Candidate Trump?

A: No.

Q: Do you have any reason to believe that she knew that Christopher Steele was doing work for you as part of that project, the opposition research on Candidate Trump?

A: No.

Q: What about Rinat Akhmetshin, did you ever talk with Rinat Akhmetshin about the fact that you were doing opposition research on Candidate Trump?

A: Not that I recall, no.

Q: Do you have any reason to believe that Christopher Steele ever spoke with Rinat Akhmetshin about the fact that Christopher Steele had been engaged by you to do work -- related to the opposition work on then Candidate Trump?

A: Do I have any reason to believe that he spoke? No, I have no reason to believe he did.

Q: Do you know if he did or not?

A: -- we've never discussed it, but I have no reason to think he would have.

Q: And if he had discussed it, would that have been consistent with the nondisclosure agreement that you would have had with Mr. Steele?

A: That would -- if he discussed it with someone like that without my knowledge, it would not have been consistent with our agreement

Q: And then given that, would it surprise you if Mr. Steele had talked with

Rinat Akhmetshin about the work related to then Candidate Trump?

A: Yes, that would surprise me.

Q: Did you discuss the fact that you were doing opposition research on Candidate Trump with anyone at Prevezon Holdings?

A: Not that I recall, no.

Q: And if you had done so, would that have been consistent with your confidentiality obligations to that client?

A: No, it wouldn't have been consistent.

Q: Did you speak with anyone at Baker Hostetler about the work that you had been engaged to do on then Candidate Trump?

A: Not that I recall.

Q: So the point in time at which you were in meetings that included -- the meetings that you had related to the Court hearing at Prevezon that you've already discussed, the dinner, the Court hearing, and then a subsequent dinner, they occur right around the same time that Natalia Veselnitskaya and Rinat Akhmetshin and the individual you described as a translator, Anatoli Samochornov, met -- or it has been reported met with individuals in the Trump campaign.

Did that topic just never come up during those three days?

A: It never came up. I don't know what else to say. It never came up.

Q: So you at the time had no idea that they were meeting with or met -- and actually, in fact, met with members of the Trump campaign (Trump Tower meeting)?

A: I didn't have any idea about that meeting until quite recently.

Q: So in an August 1, 2017 news briefing White House Press Secretary Sarah Huckabee Sanders said:

> "The Democrat linked firm Fusion GPS actually took money from the Russian government while it created the phony **dossier** that's been the basis for all of the Russia scandal fake news."

What is your response to that statement?

A: It's not true?

Q: And what in particular is not true about it?

A: Well, it's a false allegation leveled by William Browder before this committee and in other places for the purpose of his advantage. She's repeating an allegation that was aired before this committee and in other places that we were working for the Russian government and it's not true.

Most importantly the allegation that we were working for the Russian government then or ever is simply not true. I don't know what to say.

It's political rhetoric to call the dossier phony. The memos are field reports of real interviews that Chris's network conducted and there's nothing phony about it. We can argue about what's prudent and what's not, but it's not a fabrication.

Q: And I think you've already answered you contend that you were not taking money from the Russian government and that was in relation to the litigation work you had done with Baker Hostetler, correct?

A: Yes. They are a well-regarded law firm that has obligations to determine the sources of funds when they take a client and, to my knowledge, they did so and the money was not coming from the Russian government.

Q: So that was for the Prevezon work for Baker Hostetler Did you take money in any way, shape, or form that could be attributed to the Russian government for the work that you were doing -- the opposition research work that you were doing on then Candidate Trump?

A: No.

Q: Did, to the best of your knowledge, Mr. Steele take money in any way, shape, or form that could be attributed to the Russian government for the work that he did on the memos as part of the opposition research on Candidate Trump?

A: No. I'll add one more thing to the response to Sarah Huckabee Sanders, which is her assertion that we are a Democrat linked opposition research firm.

I think I addressed this earlier, but to be clear, we don't have a business of -- we're not an appendage to the Democratic party. We run a commercial business, we're all ex-journalists. We take clients from both sides of the aisle.

We have a long history of that, I'm proud of that. I'm happy to say I have lots of Republican clients and friends.

Q: To the extent there have been allegations or indications that the work that Mr. Steele did, his research into Russian interference in the 2016 election, or your work could have been influenced by Rinat Akhmetshin, do you believe that is true and if -- do you believe it's true?

A: No.

Q: Do you believe that the work that Mr. Steele did on Russian interference and possible ties to the Trump campaign or your work could have been influenced by Natalia Veselnitskaya?

A: No.

CHAPTER 21

WHAT'S NOT INCLUDED IN THE STEELE DOSSIER.

SIMPSON SAYS

We summarize those things and try to document, you know, and attach them to the underlying source material

So we sat down with a small group of reporters who were involved in investigative journalism of national security issues and we thought were in a position to make use of him (Steele) as a resource.

I think it's safe to say that, you know, at some point probably early in 2016, I had reached a conclusion about Donald Trump as a businessman and his character and I was opposed to Donald Trump.

I reached an opinion about Donald Trump and his suitability to be president of the United States and I was concerned about whether he was the best person for the job.

SIMPSON SAYS:
HE ADDED ATTACHMENTS TO THE STEELE DOSSIER

We'll go back on the record. It's 5:43 p.m.

[**NOTE**: Questions on Prevezon – not in Steele Dossier omitted]

BY MR. DAVIS:

Q: Beyond the memoranda prepared by Mr. Steele, did Fusion create any other work product relating to this investigation?

MR. LEVY: Which investigation?

MR. DAVIS: The investigation into Mr. Trump and his associates.

MR. LEVY: In addition to what?

MR. DAVIS: Sorry. The investigation into Mr. Trump and his Associates.

MR. LEVY: I'm sorry. Just repeat the whole question.

MR. DAVIS: Sure. In addition to the memoranda compiled by Mr. Steele, did Fusion itself create any other work product as part of this investigation?

MR. LEVY: I just want to make sure there's no confusion. It wasn't Fusion that created the memoranda.

MR. DAVIS: Right, but it was a subcontractor giving it back to Fusion.

MR. LEVY: That's correct.

BY MR. DAVIS:

Q: With that understanding, did Fusion create any work product of its own?

A: Yes.

Q: And can you describe what type of work product that was?

A: I believe I described it before. We do a lot of public records research, things that are in the news, things that are in court documents. **We summarize those things and try to document, you know, and attach them to the underlying source material**.

Q: So you create sort of summary memoranda of those documents?

A: Yes.

Q: Okay. And to whom is that distributed?

MR. LEVY: As a general matter?

MR. DAVIS: Well, within the course of this investigation.

MR. LEVY: Inasmuch as that answer calls for client communications the answer might be privileged, might touch on obligations

MR. FOSTER: Did you provide work product to your client?

MR. LEVY: Again, the answer to that question might implicate privilege or his obligations.

BY MR. DAVIS:

Q: Is the version of the Steele memoranda that was published by BuzzFeed identical to the version that Orbis provided Fusion?

A: To my knowledge, yes

Q: The version published by BuzzFeed contains several redactions, not merely the ones by Mr. Gubarev, G-U-B-A-R-E-V, that were later added. Were those redactions in the versions Mr. Steele provided to you?

MR. LEVY: So wait. You're asking about the version in Exhibit 3?

MR. DAVIS: Right.

MR. LEVY: And you're asking if the redactions here were delivered to Fusion?

MR. DAVIS: Right.

BY THE WITNESS [SIMPSON]:

A: No.

Q: Do you know who added those redactions?

A: No.

Q: Did any version of the memoranda list source and subsource names rather than referring to sources anonymously?

A: I'm not sure I understand the question.

Q: In the version that we have as an exhibit obviously it doesn't give identifying information for sources, it says source A, subsources, things like that. Was there ever a version that listed the actual source names rather than substituting them?

A: These are the versions that we received.

Q: They're what?

A: These are the memos that we received.

Q: Those are the memos you received. Okay.

MR. FOSTER: But he's asking if you received any other memos that listed the sources?

MR. LEVY: He did not -- what I think he said is that he did not receive any versions of these memos that listed the sources.

MR. FOSTER: Okay. Did you receive any other documentation from Mr. Steele that listed the sources?

MR. SIMPSON: I don't want to get into source information.

BY MR. DAVIS:

Q: Again, I don't want to repeat questions that have been asked, but I don't want to unintentionally omit anything. Did the version provided to the FBI include all source names?

A: I don't know that there was a version provided to the FBI.

Q: When Mr. Steele first met with the FBI in the summer of 2016 do you know if he provided the first memoranda that he created?

MR. LEVY: He's already answered that question.

BY THE WITNESS [SIMPSON]:

A: No, I don't know.

Q: Do you know if he provided any other memoranda to the FBI on a rolling basis at all at any point?

MR. LEVY: He's answered that question too.

BY THE WITNESS [SIMPSON]:

A: I don't know.

Q: So I'd like to go back to Exhibit 4, I believe. On page 3, paragraph 18 Mr. Steele's attorneys are describing the December memo and state

> "The Defendants" -- again, that's Mr. Steele and Orbis —"to receive unsolicited intelligence on the matters covered by the pre-election memoranda after the U.S. presidential election and the conclusion of the assignment for Fusion."

They reiterate this point on Exhibit 5 on page 4.　　　Request 11 asks

> "Please state whether such intelligence was actively sought by the Defendant" -- state whether such intelligence was actively sought by the second Defendant or merely received as presently pleaded." The response they say is "Such intelligence was not actively sought, it was merely received."

Did anyone -- are you aware of who sent this unsolicited intelligence to Mr. Steele?

A: No.

Q: Could you describe his (Steele's) methods of compiling the **dossier** a little more? I think before you described field interviews.

He seems to be talking about unsolicited information coming to him rather than information he sought out?

A: I can try. When you're doing field information gathering you have a network of people, sources. It's not like a light switch that you turn on and off, these are people you work with. So they call you and tell you stuff. You know, you don't close the window and stop answering phone calls, you know, when the engagement ends. So I assume this is stuff that came in straggle, whatever you call it.

Q: To the best of your knowledge, did Mr. Steele pay any of his sources or subsources in the memoranda for information?

A: I don't know. I think there's been a little bit of confusion I would like to clear up. Some people were saying that he was paying people for information. I don't know whether he does or not, but that's not basically how I understand field operations to work.

You commission people to gather information for you rather than sort of paying someone for a document or to sit for an interview or something like that. That's not how I understand it works.

Q: To make sure I understand, are you saying you don't pay for particular information, you would have an established financial arrangement with someone?

A: If he did at all, but I did not ask and he did not share that information. He did not invoice me for any such.

Q: Did Mr. Steele ever discuss his opinion of Mr. Trump with you?

A: We didn't discuss our political views of Mr. Trump, I don't think, at least not that I specifically remember, if that's what you mean.

Q: That is. If I recall correctly, you said earlier that once Fusion had exhausted public documentary sources you turned to Mr. Steele and some other subcontractors for human intelligence; is that correct?

A: Yeah, field intelligence.

Q: Would your engagement with your client have ended had you not turned to human intelligence?

A: I have no idea. I mean, I can't speculate.

Q: Well, to clarify, when say you had exhausted the public documentation, are you saying you reached the end of your work or was there still more?

A: No. It's a broad project, there's lots of things going on. We're pulling legal filings and bankruptcies and all sorts of other stuff on all kinds of issues. I was talking about specific lines of inquiry.

Q: To the best of your knowledge, do Rinat Akhmetshin and Christopher Steele know each other?

A: I don't know.

Q: To the best of your knowledge, has Mr. Akhmetshin worked with Orbis?

A: Not to my knowledge.

MR. FOSTER: If Mr. Akhmetshin were one of the sources in the **dossier**, would you know that?

MR. SIMPSON: I believe he would have told me that by now given the public controversy over this matter, but he hasn't.

BY MR. DAVIS: I'm sorry. Is the "he" --

A: Chris Steele.

Q: How often would you say you interacted with Mr. Akhmetshin during the 2016 elections season?

A: Infrequently, intermittently.

Q: When was the last time you spoke with him?

A: I don't remember, but I don't think it was -- I just don't remember.

Q: To the best of your knowledge, was **Ed Lieberman** aware of your Trump research project?

A: Not to the best of my knowledge.

MORE ON THE MAINSTREAM MEDIA

MR. FOSTER: Could you just tell us generally who else other than your client was aware of the Trump research project as it was going on...who else knew that you were doing it?

MR. SIMPSON: Journalists.

MR. FOSTER: In the summer of 2016?

MR. SIMPSON: Yes.

MR. FOSTER: And they knew that because you were telling them about it?

MR. SIMPSON: We get calls from journalists who are working on stories about all kinds of subjects and some things we can answer questions on and others we don't. I'm a former journalist, as I think you know, and we do lots of different kinds of research and people who are working on a story will call us and say what do you know about, you know, **Carter Page** and we'll say, well, here's the things that we know.

MR. FOSTER: They're aware you're being paid to do that research for a client?

MR. SIMPSON: I don't know. Generally that's not an issue.

MR. FOSTER: So my question was who knew that you were doing the research, the Trump-Russia research at the time?

MR. LEVY: He answered the question. He told you he spoke with journalists and told them what he had found.

MR. FOSTER: Right. I was trying to clarify. My question was whether or not they knew you were being paid to do that research.

MR. LEVY: He answered that question too and he said he did not explain that to the journalists.

MR. SIMPSON: It's hard to generalize.   I run a business, it's a research business. Reporters know we have clients who pay us to do research. So, you know, I don't remember any specific queries about whether we were being paid or not, but **I think most journalists would assume that someone had paid us to do research.**

MR. FOSTER: They knew you were doing a Trump oppo research project as opposed to a Hillary Clinton oppo research project?

MR. LEVY: From 2015 through the end of the election?

MR. FOSTER: Can you let the witness answer, please.

MR. SIMPSON: The word "they" is extremely broad. Journalists would call and ask questions about specific things and from that they might conclude that we were doing a Trump oppo project.

It's just worth pointing out that in a political season all kinds of people are doing research on all kinds of things.

Some people are interested in trade, other people are interested in guns. So you wouldn't necessarily intuit exactly what we were doing. Most people are interested in, you know -- they're interested in the story they're working on. So some people will say, hey, I'm interested in whether Donald Trump gets his ties from third-world countries and they wouldn't ask about anything else.

BY MR. DAVIS:

Q: You mentioned before, if I recall correctly, that Fusion was having issues with persons attempting to hack it?

A: That's a current concern, yes.

Q: When did that concern -- when did you first become aware of that concern?

A: Relatively recently.

Q: So after the election?

A: Yes.

MR. FOSTER: Did you tell journalists that you had engaged Mr. Steele in the summer of 2016?

MR. SIMPSON: I don't specifically remember doing that until the fall.

MR. FOSTER: After the election or before?

MR. SIMPSON: Before the election.

MR. FOSTER: Can you remember the context in which you told them that?

MR. SIMPSON: Yes.

MR. FOSTER: Can you describe it for us, please?

MR. SIMPSON: Sure. Essentially there was -- at some point the controversy over the Trump campaign's possible relationship with the Kremlin became, you know, one of the main -- major issues in the campaign and there were things that Chris knew and understood to be the case that only he could really explain in a credible way, and I thought that -- we thought that he should be the one that explains them, you know.

So we sat down with a small group of reporters who were involved in

investigative journalism of national security issues and we thought were in a position to make use of him (Steele) as a resource.

MR. FOSTER: Do you recall whether that was before or after he ended his relationship with the FBI?

MR. SIMPSON: Before.

BY MR. DAVIS:

Q: Do you recall what the first published article -- when the first published article came out that referenced material from the memoranda?

A: Not specifically.

MR. FOSTER: Earlier you talked about evaluating the credibility of the information in the memoranda that you were being provided by Mr. Steele and, by way of summary, you talked about your belief that he was credible and that you had worked with him before and the information he had provided you had been reliable in the past. Did you take any steps to try to assess the credibility of his sources, his unnamed sources in the material that he was providing to you?

MR. SIMPSON: Yes, but I'm not going to get into sourcing information.

MR. FOSTER: So without getting into naming the sources or anything like that, what steps did you take to try to verify their credibility?

MR. SIMPSON: I'm going to decline to answer that.

MR. FOSTER: Why?

MR. LEVY: It's a voluntary interview, and in addition to that he wants to be very careful to protect his sources.

Somebody's already been killed as a result of the publication of this dossier and no harm should come to anybody related to this honest work.

MR. FOSTER: I'm not asking him to identify the sources. I'm just asking what steps he took to try to verify or validate the information.

MR. LEVY: He's given you --

MR. FOSTER: If he can answer generally without identifying the sources, I'd ask him to answer.

MR. LEVY: He's given you over nine hours of information and he's going to decline to answer this one question.

MR. FOSTER: And several others.

MR. LEVY: Not many.

BY MR. DAVIS:

Q: I think you mentioned that you were in London when you first heard that someone was interested in hiring Fusion to work on the Trump research; is that correct?

MR. LEVY: Repeat the question.

MR. DAVIS: If I recall correctly, Mr. Simpson said that he was in London when he first heard that somebody was interested in hiring Fusion to do Trump research?

BY THE WITNESS [SIMPSON]:

A: That's my recollection.

Q: Were either of the clients on this project not American citizens?

A: Were either of the clients on this --

MR. LEVY: Clients on which project?

BY MR. DAVIS:

Q: Were any clients on the Trump research not American citizens?

A: I don't mind answering that if that's okay. **They're domestic clients.**

MR. FOSTER: You said earlier that the information that you gather in your work is owned by the client, it's not owned by you, and so therefore you also referenced your nondisclosure agreements and that you felt like if you had information that related to national security or law enforcement that the nondisclosure agreement did not prevent you from disclosing that information to third parties. Is that a fair summary?

MR. LEVY: Wait. You said a lot there. Which third parties are you talking about?

MR. FOSTER: Well, to law enforcement.

MR. LEVY: I think he's answered this. You're asking him whether it was permittable under his contractual obligations to report a crime to the national security community, and he said yes, it's fine for him to do that.

MR. FOSTER: Right. I'm trying to summarize the previous answer as a premise to my next question. Is that an accurate summary of what you said before?

MR. LEVY: Summarizing testimony is dangerous after he's given nine hours of it. If you want to ask him a question, ask him a question.

MR. FOSTER: Is there a specific provision in your NDA that provides an exception for disclosure to law enforcement or intelligence agencies?

MR. LEVY: I think he earlier didn't talk about the contract, but if you want to talk about it as a matter of practice what your understanding is, go ahead.

MR. SIMPSON: I don't know.

MR. FOSTER: My colleague Ms. Sawyer asked you earlier about public reports that the initial client on the Trump work was a Republican and that it's also been publicly reported that later there was another client who was a supporter of Hillary Clinton.

Are you the source for any of those public reports?

MR. LEVY: A hundred percent of what you were saying was referring to news articles, right.

MR. SIMPSON: I've been asked about this by various journals as to what I've heard, whether they can report things that they've heard elsewhere, and I have not -- I don't know if you'd classify that as being a source, but I've been asked those questions and I've avoiding getting into specifics. But I have -- if people have accurate information of a general nature like that, I generally would not -- I would confirm things.

MR. FOSTER: Sorry. I didn't understand your answer.

MR. MUSE: It's quite clear.

MR. SIMPSON: Depends on what you say a source is.

If someone calls me and say I hear client No. 1 was a Republican, then I'd say I don't have any problem with you writing that. That's not quite the same thing.

MR. FOSTER: So you confirm the accuracy of information?

MR. LEVY: He didn't say that.

MR. SIMPSON: There are certain things that I've chosen not to deny. You know, generally speaking, I deal with a lot of journalists. I'm not going to mislead people.

BY MR. DAVIS:

Q: To the extent you can clarify, is it that there were two sets of clients, one of whom was Republican and one of which was a Clinton supporter, or was it one person's whose views changed?

MR. LEVY: We're not going to get into the identity of clients. As you know, we've agreed to an interview about questions 5 through 13 of the March 24 request.

Questions 1 - 4 talk about the identities of the clients. The Chair and the Ranking Member agreed with counsel for Mr. Simpson about the scope of this interview and that question is outside of it. In addition, the answer to that question would implicate privilege and obligations.

He's talked to you for nine hours, he's given you a lot of information, and he's not going to answer questions about identities of clients.

MR. DAVIS: You've asserted attorney-client work product privilege --

MR. LEVY: There is no such privilege. I've asserted the attorney work product privilege, we've asserted privileges under the First Amendment, we've asserted the attorney-client privilege, and we've asserted privileges of confidentiality. It's a voluntary interview and he's declining to answer the question.

MR. DAVIS: I understand that.

Q: So with the Prevezon matter, then, is it correct the law firm involved was Baker Hostetler and the ultimate client was Prevezon, is that right, while you were working there?

A: Yes.

Q: So any attorney-client privileges within the context of that would be – the holder of that privilege is Prevezon; is that correct?

MR. LEVY: That's a legal conclusion that he's not qualified to draw.

MR. DAVIS: You don't feel that you can speak to it without their permission?

MR. LEVY: Speak to what?

MR. DAVIS: To questions that would be covered by attorney-client privilege.

MR. LEVY: I'm not sure he's qualified to answer that question.

BY MR. DAVIS:

Q: Did you work with any law firms in relation to the Trump investigation?

MR. LEVY: Again, we're not getting into the identity of any clients --

MR. DAVIS: I didn't say client.

MR. LEVY: I understand. Or their lawyers.

MR. FOSTER: I think the issue we're trying to deal with is in order to assess your claims of privilege the committee needs to understand at least as much about the context of the **dossier** work as it does about the Prevezon work in terms of who was involved. So if there's a law firm involved … then we need to be able to assess whether or not that was in anticipation of litigation, whether he was doing it by the direction of a law firm in order to assess your assertions of privilege.

MR. LEVY: I understand. We've identified our position. We've been talking -- Mr. Simpson has been answering your questions since 9:30 this morning, it's now 6:15. He's been fully cooperative and he's here because the Chair and the Ranking Member agreed to a limited scope. The questions you're asking are outside of that scope and this is part of why appearing at a hearing was going to be impossible.

Through this agreement we're here. He's given you a ton of information. If you want to discuss the privilege with counsel after the interview, you may do so. He's answered a ton of questions today and he's going to decline to answer this last one.

MR. FOSTER: The last one did you work with a law firm on the Trump matter?

MR. LEVY: He's declining to answer.

MR. FOSTER: There were several points in the interview where you made a point of saying your firm is not a Democratic linked firm in reference to the Sarah Huckabee Sanders quote.

It's been publicly reported that you did opposition research for a client targeting Mr. Romney in the 2012 election.

Have you ever done opposition research regarding Mr. Obama?

MR. LEVY: We're not going to get into specific client matters that are outside the scope of this interview. He's told you he's represented clients on the right and left, but he's not going to get into other matters beyond Prevezon and what he did in the 2016 election.

MR. SIMPSON: **I did investigate Senator Obama's campaign in 2008 when I was working for the Wall Street Journal and wrote an article that caused his campaign chair to resign.**

The record is replete -- or the public report of my work is replete with examples of investigations I've done of Democrats that resulted in them losing their elections and being prosecuted.

MR. LEVY: At the Wall Street Journal?

MR. SIMPSON: Yes.

BY MR. DAVIS:

Q: Are you party to a joint defense agreement related to Prevezon work?

MR. LEVY: He's not going to talk about privileged discussions or agreements, and he's probably not qualified to answer anyway.

BY MR. DAVIS:

Q: Is Fusion GPS paying Cunningham Levy for the firm's representation of you or as a third party?

MR. LEVY: **That's privileged also.** He's not getting into payments to his lawyers and it's beyond the scope of this interview.

BY MR. DAVIS:

Q: Has Fusion GPS ever offered directly or indirectly to pay journalists to publish information?

A: No.

Q: Are you aware of any Fusion clients offering directly or indirectly to pay journalists to publish information from Fusion?

MR. LEVY: **While working for Fusion on a Fusion matter or as a general matter?**

MR. FOSTER: Can you let the witness answer.

MR. LEVY: Well, if the question's clear he can answer any question --

MR. FOSTER: I think the question was clear.

MR. LEVY: -- within the scope of the interview --

MR. DAVIS: Are there any of Fusion's clients offering --

THE (TRANSCRIPTION) REPORTER: Guys.

BY MR. DAVIS:

Q: I'll repeat the question. Are you aware of any of Fusion's clients offering directly or indirectly to pay journalists to publish information from Fusion?

A: Not to my knowledge or recollection, no.

MR. FOSTER: What was the end date of the Trump engagement?

MR. LEVY: He told you he didn't recall.

MR. SIMPSON: That's not correct. The election was the end date. I assume you're asking about the general election? The election date would have been the end.

MR. FOSTER: So you didn't do any work on the Trump matter after the election date, that was the end of your work?

MR. SIMPSON: I had no client after the election.

MR. FOSTER: It's 6:21. Let's go off the record for a minute.

(A short break was had.)

SIMPSON SAYS:
"I WAS OPPOSED TO TRUMP"

BY MS. SAWYER: We'll go back on the record. It's 6:30.

Q: We appreciate your time today, your patience in answering our questions. You've been asked a number of questions just about -- well, strike that. Were any of the particular factual findings or conclusions that you reached with regard to the research that was being done related to Russian interference in the 2016 election including possible ties to the Trump campaign, were any of the factual findings or conclusions influenced in any way by the identity of the client for whom you were doing that work?

A: All the questions you've asked I guess this one I've not given a lot of thought to. Offhand, not that I can think of.

Q: So you weren't trying to reach a particular conclusion based on the identity had they asked you to find -- well, strike that.

I think what I'm trying to get some sense of comfort around is to the extent there might be concerns that the work being done was driven in a direction designed to reach a particular conclusion for a client or because of the client's identity was that the case?

A: I think it's safe to say that, you know, at some point probably early in 2016 I had reached a conclusion about Donald Trump as a businessman and his character and

I was opposed to Donald Trump.

I'm not going to pretend that that wouldn't have entered into my thinking. You know, again, I was a journalist my whole life. So we were, you know, trained not to take sides and practiced in not taking sides.

So most of what I do as a research person is we try to avoid getting into situations where one's etiology or political views would cloud your work because it's a known hazard, but, you know,

I reached an opinion about Donald Trump and his suitability to be president of the United States and I was concerned about whether he was the best person for the job.

Q: And given that you had been trained not to allow etiology to cloud your work, it sounds like you reached a conclusion and had concerns about Candidate Trump.

What steps did you take to then ensure that your conclusion didn't cloud the work that was being done?

A: Well, to be clear, my concerns were in the category of character and competence rather than -- I didn't have any specific concerns for much of the time about his views, which I don't share, but that wasn't really the issue.

Most of what we do has to do with do people have integrity and whether they've been involved in illicit activity. So those were the things I focused on.

Q: So the conclusion that you reached, was it informed by the research that you were — your personal conclusion, was it informed by the research that you were conducting?

A: Yes. We deal in factual information and over the course of this project we gathered lots of facts about Donald Trump.

SIMPSON SAYS:
TRUMP'S INTEGRITY HIS CONCERN

Q: You mentioned that earlier and I think you made clear a number of times in the course of the day that the specific work on Russian interference and possible ties to the campaign that Mr. Steele was doing was one part of that bigger picture, and I did want to ask you about some of that bigger picture of the work and get a sense from you, if I could, you know, some of the background and findings.

In particular one of the things you had mentioned -- well, you just mentioned right now as we were speaking the term "illicit activity."

What, if any, research did you conduct that gave you any concerns about then Candidate Trump and potential illicit activity?

A: I think the thing I cited to you was his relationship with organized crime figures, and that was a concern.

For the Forgotten Americans

Q: And what can you share with us about the findings, your findings?

A: I've tried to share as much as I could think of over the course of today.

As I say, there were various allegations of fraudulent business practices or dishonest business practices or connections with organized crime figures.

In fact, you know, there was numerous others that I can't remember the names of. It was a long history of associations with people accused of involvement in criminal activity.

You know, just to reiterate, the facts of these investigations are the facts and we don't try to drive an investigation to any particular conclusion, certainly not based on our political views.

So I think it would be, you know, not believable for me to tell you I didn't reach, you know, views about Donald Trump's integrity, but, you know, those were -- those didn't influence the research in terms of the findings. Those were the findings.

Q: You mentioned specifically and I think with regard to organized crime particularly ties to Felix Sater is one. You indicated a connection to Yudkovich Mogilebich, I think it is.

A: Mogilebich.

Q: Mogilebich, which we can spell for you. Tell me if I have this correct. M-O-G-I-L-E-B-I-C-H.

A: Yes.

MR. SIMPSON: Semyon, S-E-M-Y-O-N.

BY MS. SAWYER:

Q: Yudkovich, did I get that –

A: I believe I was probably talking fast and I think I might have made a reference to Yanukovych, which is the former president of the Ukraine.

Q: With regard to any of that work, did you create work product based on that work?

A: I don't specifically recall what we would have created.

Q: And with regard to that work, did you share any of that information with law enforcement agencies?

A: No. I mean, just to reiterate, the only contact that, you know, occurred during this engagement was -- at least to my knowledge, was Chris's dealing with the FBI. Other than that, I don't remember having any dealings with the FBI.

Q: You had also mentioned earlier in the day work -- that there was an investigation about money from Kazakhstan?

A: Yes.

Q: And could you tell me about what you investigated and what you learned?

A: There was some parallel litigation in New York involving attempts by the government of Kazakhstan to recover money that had been allegedly stolen from Kazakhstan, billions of dollars in a colossal bank failure. The name of the bank was BTA Bank.

It's been well established in various courts that the government's allegations are basically true, which is that large amounts of money were illicitly removed from this bank, laundered across Europe and into the United States apparently. **Allegedly.**

So there was a civil case, at least one civil case in New York involving -- filed by the city of Almaty, A-L-M-A-T-Y, against some alleged Kazakh money launderers I don't remember exactly how, but we learned that -- it wasn't from Chris.

We learned that Felix Sater had some connections with these people, and it's been more recently in the media that he's helping the government of Kazakhstan to recover this money. There's been media reports that the money went into the Trump Soho or it went into the company that built the Trump Soho. I can't remember the name.

Q: So the connection in that instance was to Felix Sater and through Felix Sater to -- potentially to Donald Trump?

A: Yes. It was a company that Felix Sater and Donald Trump were involved in together.

Q: And the research you did on that project, was that public source research? Did you have any other – did you have human intelligence sources on that project?

A: I think I probably did have some human sources. That's my answer.

Q: And did you use subcontractors at all on that work?

A: I can't say specifically whether it was -- I remember commissioning some public record-type research on Sater and his history in New York.

Q: Did you feel in the course of that that you had uncovered evidence of any criminal activity by Donald Trump?

A: In the course of that I don't think so. I think my concern was the associations with known organized crime figures.

Q: And that included Felix Sater?

A: Yes.

Q: Anyone else in particular?

A: There were others.

MR. LEVY: Beyond what we've discussed today?

MS. SAWYER: Yes, beyond what we've already discussed.

BY THE WITNESS [SIMPSON]:

A: Another figure involved in the Trump Soho project was a central Asian person named Arif, A-R-I-F, is the last name.

The first name is generally spelled Tevfik, it's T-E-V-F-I-K.

If you search under a different transiteration of that name you can find open source reporting alleging that he's an organized crime figure from Central Asia and he had an arrest for involvement in child prostitution.

Q: You mentioned as well that you had reviewed tax bills. Were these specifically Donald Trump's tax bills?

A: They were Trump properties and I believe we may have reviewed some public information about estate taxes and things like that. We didn't have access to his tax returns.

Q: Did you reach any conclusions based on your review of his tax bills? I think you mentioned that in connection with trying to assess either financial connections or his financial standing. Did you reach any conclusions with regard to either of those?

A: Yes. I concluded -- we concluded that his statements about what individual properties were worth were greatly exaggerated and at odds with the information that he'd supplied, you know, in legal filings with tax authorities and other records, corporate records.

Q: Did any of that indicate anything that showed a connection to Russia or the Russian government or Russian officials or Russian oligarchs?

A: Not that I can recall.

Q: You mentioned as well, you brought up Trump golf courses. What in particular were you looking into with regard to Donald Trump's golf courses?

A: The original inquiry was into the value of the courses, whether he had to borrow money to buy them, whether they were encumbered with debt, how much money they brought in, what valuations he put on them, and property tax filings.

Q: And in general can you share what findings and conclusions you reached?

MR. LEVY: With regard to?

MS. SAWYER: To the work on the golf properties.

BY THE WITNESS [SIMPSON]:

A: A number of them don't make any money. His valuations of the properties are questionable. I guess those would be the main findings.

Q: You just mentioned broadly but didn't describe it, you mentioned research on Scotland. I don't know if it was particular properties or something with regard to Scotland. Can you just describe what that research was.

A: Sure. He has golf courses in Scotland and Ireland and one of the facets of UK or Anglo company law is that private companies have to file financial statements, public financial statements.

So when you're looking at a guy like Donald Trump who doesn't like to share information about his company, it's useful to find a jurisdiction where he's required to share that information with the local government.

So we went and ordered the records — the financial statements of the golf courses. There's also a long-running land use controversy -- I think there's multiple long-running land use controversies over those properties. We haven't really touched on this at all, but there were also environmental issues that were part of the research.

Q: With regard to the public financial statements, did you reach any conclusions based on that?

A: That they were not profitable entities. I don't specifically recall. I just remember that these were not doing very well and that he'd sunk a lot of money into them and he hadn't gotten a lot of money back yet.

MS. QUINT: You mentioned a couple of times, Mr. Simpson, that you had particular familiarity with Mr. Manafort and even that you were more familiar with him in particular than Chris Steele was. In general and it might not be easy to be general about it, but what was your focus when you had looked into Manafort? What main areas were you familiar with?

MR. SIMPSON: Over the years, originally at the Wall Street Journal we learned of his relationship with Ukrainian and Russian oligarchs. So it was generally continued in that vein. He was subject of some litigation over his business dealings in New York. There was a lawsuit filed by the opposition politician from Ukraine accusing him of involvement in corruption in Ukraine.

So as just a -- not for any particular client, but just because these matters are something I follow I had collected those documents. I think there's probably some other litigation that I collected that was in a similar vein.

MS. QUINT: And it was all documentary or did you have human sources for your Manafort research?

MR. SIMPSON: I don't think -- for the most part it was just what you call gathering string, just accumulating files on people or subjects that are of interest.

BY MS. SAWYER:

Q: The committee, certain members of the committee, the Chairman and Ranking Member along with Senators Graham and Whitehouse had sent a request for documents and information on July 19.

I understand your efforts to identify that information are ongoing and I know that in response to one of my questions about Mr. Page your attorney has already said that the request for information is pending and being reviewed. I just wanted to ask you a couple of questions about some of the other individuals that we had identified in that letter and in particular in No. 6?

MR. LEVY: Do you have an exhibit or should I just get my copy out?

MS. SAWYER: I'm happy to enter it as an exhibit or I can just read the names. I don't think there's any reason we need to --

MR. LEVY: Just read the names to move it along, that's fine.

MS. SAWYER: I don't think there's any reason -- there's nothing in this letter to inform your answer otherwise.

Q: So with regard to Alpha Group, sometimes I've heard Alpha Group, sometimes I've heard Alpha Bank. I don't know if they're two distinct entities. Do you know anything about Alpha Bank or Alpha Group with regard to Russian interference in the 2016 election?

A: Alpha Group is not a corporate person, it's not an entity. It's just a collective name. Alpha Bank is a bank. I know a limited amount. I know, you know, journalists were working on issues related to this and they asked us about it, but the information didn't come from us.

Q: So you were asked by journalists about it, but you're saying whatever information you had was not generated by Fusion GPS?

A: That's right. I know they're a big player and they have long, deep ties to Vladimir Putin. One of the founders, Pyotr Aven, P-Y-O-T-R, second word Aven, A-V-E-N, was an associate of Vladimir Putin when he was in the mayor's office in Saint Petersburg around the time same that Bill Browder was doing business with the mayor's office.

They're very powerful politically and economically in Russia and they have -- in the tens of billions are the assets of the founders and they have all sorts of interests. They have epic disputes with western corporations, including BP. So people in my business tend to just have a lot of institutional knowledge about them and, you know, I shared my institutional knowledge about them.

Q: You mentioned other founders. Are those other founders Mikhail Fridman and German Khan?

A: Yes.

Q: Do you have any information there have been reports about potential communications between a server at Alpha Bank and potentially servers that belong to the Trump organization or Trump – some entity associated with Donald Trump? Do you have any information about those particular reports?

A: That's kind of an open-ended question. I think what I said is we were asked about that and it wasn't -- that information wasn't generated by us and I'm happy to say it's beyond our competence to have generated, but in the course of being asked about it, you know, people gave us information. If you don't know what else to say.

Q: And what information were you given?

A: A bunch of data. I mean, we were shown like do you know what this would mean, does this mean, and it's beyond -- it's really -- it's certainly beyond my competence.

Q: So the data that you were shown, you could not draw any conclusions from it?

A: I did not draw any conclusions from the data.

Q: Another individual that there's been a lot of press reporting on is Sergei Millian. Other than what -- what, if anything, can you tell us about did you conduct any research into Mr. Millian? And, if so, what conclusions did you reach with regard to Russian interference in the 2016 election?

A: We learned from sources that he had connections to the Trump organization and we did an open source investigation of him. We found a picture of him with Donald Trump and another real estate investor in Florida.

We've discovered that's not his real name or at least not the name he came to the United States with and that before he became a real estate broker he was a linguist and translator.

Speaking generally, people with advanced training in linguistics are oftentimes involved in intelligence matters, but I don't know whether he is or isn't. Various reporters became interested in him because he was boasting about his connections to the Trump organization in the Trump campaign.

So we got lots of inquiries about who was he, was he a spy, you know, that sort of thing.

Q: And did you make a determination whether or not he had actual ties to the Trump campaign?

A: Well, some of the -- yes. I mean, he was -- I think he's Facebook friends with Michael Cohen. I'm sorry. It was some social media connection. It was either Twitter friends or Facebook friends.

It was public information. We took it from that that they did know each other. I guess we gradually learned of Michael Cohen's role in the Trump campaign as opposed to in the Trump organization.

Q: And what did you learn about Cohen's role in the Trump campaign?

A: We learned that his job included dealing with inquiries about Russia and he seemed to get all of the serious inquiries, investigative inquiries about Russia. He seemed to know a lot about that.

We learned that he was a very intimidating person who had a history of threatening reporters with libel suits.

We learned that he's married to -- his father-in-law is a Ukrainian emigre, that he had some Ukrainian clients and connections to the taxi industry in New York which is heavily populated with Russian emigres, and we learned that he was involved in some of Trump's projects where there was a lot of Russian buyers. The only other thing I can think of is that he was also the person who dealt with allegations against Mr. Trump from the tabloids.

Q: And with regard to Trump projects with Russian buyers, what specific projects had a number of Russian buyers?

A: I don't specifically remember. Florida maybe. I think it was Florida. Sorry.

MS. SAWYER: Just give us a minute. I think that's really all of our questions. I don't know if there's follow-up that you all had.

MR. FOSTER: Just very quickly. I can do it from here. So I asked you -- or you were asked earlier about representations that you're not --

you don't see your firm as being Democrat linked and in my previous question I asserted that there had been public reports that you had done work, opposition research during the 2012 election aimed at Mr. Romney, but I didn't ask you to confirm that. Is that correct?

MR. LEVY: Work for clients outside the scope of the interview is not within the scope of the interview.

MR. FOSTER: It's relevant to his claim that he's not a Democrat linked firm.

MR. LEVY: He's answered that question.

He's given you multiple answers to that question and significant information in support of his answer to that question, and that small fact which may or may not be pertinent is that he's going to decline to answer because it's outside the scope of this interview.

MR. SIMPSON: I decline to answer.

MR. FOSTER: In some of the questioning in the last round there was some talk of your – you didn't have a particular aim in your research, you were following the facts wherever they lead.

Is it fair to say -- is it a fair description to say that your job was opposition research aimed at Mr. Trump? That's been widely reported and characterized that way. Do you think that's a fair characterization of what your job was?

MR. LEVY: He's been talking for nine and a half hours, a lot of which was describing his work. To simplify it in any particular way at this point I think is unfair to the witness.

MR. FOSTER: You weren't hired to find positive information about Mr. Trump, were you?

MR. SIMPSON: To the contrary. I think when you're doing research on any subject you're trying to figure out what the truth is. So if Donald Trump's got a good business record and he's really worth billions of dollars, that's important information.

In fact, you shouldn't be feeding reporters stories about how Donald Trump is not worth billions of dollars if he's worth billions of dollars.

So, you know, I think the connotation of negativity, I get, you know, where you're coming from, but, in fact, you're just trying to figure out what's true.

It's like with the Prevezon case, we were trying to figure out who's telling the truth, is it our guys or is it Browder. I do my job well and I get rehired when I give them the right information, when I give them accurate information. **So if Donald Trump turned out to be a great businessman, that's what I would have to tell people.**

MR. FOSTER: Nothing further from me.

MR. LEVY: Before we go off the record, will we be entitled to a copy of the transcript?

MR. FOSTER: You'll be able to review the transcript and request corrections, make an errata.

MR. LEVY: Will it be kept confidential? We'd like to make a request that it be kept confidential given the sensitivity of the matters discussed today.

MR. FOSTER: Your request is noted.

MR. LEVY: Noted, but no decision on it?

MR. FOSTER: No decision.

MR. LEVY: And upon reviewing the transcript, when will we have that opportunity?

MR. FOSTER: We can arrange that off the record.

MR. LEVY: When we do we just reserve the right obviously to correct the record or supplement it.

MR. FOSTER: That's why we'd allow you to review it.

MR. LEVY: Thank you very much.

MR. DAVIS: Nothing further. We're going off the record at 7:04.

(Whereupon the interview was concluded at 7:04 p.m.)

APPENDIX

SENATE JUDICIARY COMMITTEE - U.S. SENATE

WASHINGTON, D.C.

INTERVIEW OF: GLENN SIMPSON

TUESDAY, AUGUST 22, 2017

The interview in this matter was held at

the Hart Senate Office Building, commencing at 9:34 a.m.

APPEARANCES:

SENATE JUDICIARY COMMITTEE:

Patrick Davis, Deputy Chief Investigative Counsel, Chairman Grassley

Jason Foster, Chief Investigative Counsel, Chairman Grassley

Samantha Brennan, Investigative Counsel, Chairman Grassley

Daniel Parker, Investigative Assistant, Chairman Grassley

Joshua Flynn-Brown, Investigative Counsel, Chairman Grassley

Scott Graber, Legislative Assistant/Counsel, Senator Graham

Heather Sawyer, Chief Oversight Counsel, Senator Feinstein

Jennifer Duck, Staff Director, Senator Feinstein

Molly Claflin, Counsel, Senator Feinstein

Lara Quint, Chief Counsel, Senator Whitehouse

FOR THE WITNESS:

Joshua Levy, Cunningham Levy Muse

Robert Muse, Cunningham Levy Muse

Rachel Clattenburg, Cunningham Levy Muse

APPENDIX

UNCLASSIFIED, COMMITTEE SENSITIVE

**EXECUTIVE SESSION
PERMANENT SELECT COMMITTEE ON INTELLIGENCE,
U.S. HOUSE OF REPRESENTATIVES,
WASHINGTON, D.C.**

INTERVIEW OF: GLENN SIMPSON
Tuesday, November14, 2017
Washington, D.C.
The interview in the above matter was held in Room HVC-304, the Capitol, commencing at 2:13 p.m.

PRESENT:
Representatives Conaway, King, Rooney, Ros-Lehtinen, Gowdy, Schiff, Himes, Speier, Quigley, Swalwell, Castro, and Heck .

APPEARANCES:

For the PERMANENT SELECT COMMITTEE ON INTELLIGENCE:
ALL NAMES REDACTED

For GLENN SIMPSON:
ROBERT F. MUSE, ESQ.
JOSHUA LEVY, ESQ.
RACHELCLATTENBURG,ESQ.
UNCLASSIFIED, COMMITTEE SENSITIVE

ABOUT THE AUTHOR

Daniel David Elles ("Danny") lived overseas (Europe, Hong Kong and Singapore) for fifteen years. He and Elvis, his beloved Pug, live in Sterling Heights, Michigan. He's the author of Social Media Serial Killer. And, he writes the award winning children's series: "The Adventures of Elvis the Pug." They visit 5,000 children every year for National Reading Month and at Hospitals.

He was a second founding member of Sequent (acquired by IBM), first international director at NetLabs (acquired by Seagate), first international director for China's largest computer company (Stone: Beijing), Mercury Asia-Pacific (acquired by HP) and Director for Fortune 500 companies: Unisys Hong Kong and Ogilvy & Mather (Singapore).

He attended Assumption Grotto and St. Jude in Detroit, Michigan. He was captain of St. Clair High School's Hall of Fame football team, an elected Executive Council member of the Delta Chi Fraternity at Michigan State University and a graduate of the prestigious United States Marine Corp's (USMC) Officer Candidates School, Platoon Leaders Class (PLC), at Quantico.

After returning State-side, he served on the Board of Directors for various charities (i.e. the local chapters for ALS and Habitat for Humanity) and the quasi-government Clinton Township Downtown Development Authority (DDA). He also tutored Hispanic families at Macomb Literacy Partners and ushered at Mt. Clemens's St. Peters Church. In 2010, he qualified to run for State Representative – as an "Independent" – in the 31st District of Michigan's House of Representatives.

THANKS FOR READING AND I HOPE YOU ENJOYED.

Again, please contact me for any corrections, updates, concerns, or whatever you may have.

PLEASE FEEL FREE TO CONTACT ME:

Website:	www.DanielDavidElles.com
	www.TiberPublishing.com
Email:	Daniel.David.Elles@gmail.com
	Daniel@TiberPublishing.com
Facebook:	@TIBERBOOKS
Twitter:	@TIBERBOOKS

TIBER PUBLISHING:

400 Renaissance Center   Suite 2600

Detroit, MI 48243

TEL   1.888.888.2171   FAX: 1.313.692.6469

$15.99

ISBN 978-0-9968863-7-6

51599>

9 780996 886376

Library of Congress: 2018909559
ISBN-10:   0996886370
ISBN-13:   9780996886376

Made in the USA
Coppell, TX
10 December 2019

12711058R00115